ISBN 978-81-909760-4-6

Cows Are Cool
Love 'em!

By
Dr. Sahadeva dasa

B.com., ACA., ICWA., PhD
Chartered Accountant

Soul Science University Press

www.cowism.com

"...the gentle, large-brained, social cow, that caresses our hands and face with her rough tongue, and is more like man's sister than any other non-human being—the majestic, beautiful creature with the Juno eyes..." -W. H. Hudson

---

Readers interested in the subject matter of this book are invited to correspond with the publisher at : **SoulScienceUniversity@gmail.com**
Ph.: +91 98490 95990

First Edition: December 2009

Published by   : **Dr. Sahadeva dasa** (SoulScienceUniversity@gmail.com)

                      for Soul Science University Press

Designed by   : **Sri Sailesh Ijmulwar**
                      waar creatives, Hyderabad

Printed by   : **Rainbow Print Pack**
                      Hyderabad.

"Just see Krishna's picture, how He's loving the cow. You see? He is instructing by His practical life how He is compassionate with the cows. Krishna is always associated with cows and His devotees. In pictures Krishna is always seen with cows and His associates such as the cowherd boys and the gopis. Krishna, the Supreme Personality of Godhead, cannot be alone.

Just like we have got some hobbies, we keep some cats and dogs, Krishna has got also hobby. What is that? Surabhir abhipalayantam [Bs. 5.29]. He's always engaged in taking care of the surabhi cows. Gopala. That is His business. So He's so simple, life.

So it appears that how much strictly the cow protection was there so that the gavah, payasodhasvatir muda. They were... You'll see Krishna. He is always with cows, and how the cows look very happy with Krishna. And Krishna is personally teaching how to protect cows. He became a cowherd boy."

-Srila Prabhupada

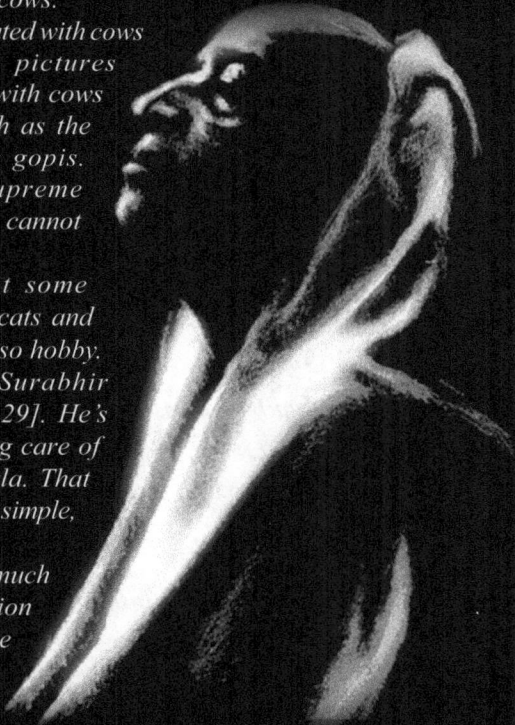

By The Same Author

Oil-Final Countdown To A Global Crisis And Its Solutions

End of Modern Civilization And Alternative Future

To Kill Cow Means To End Human Civilization

Cow And Humanity - Made For Each Other

Cows Are Cool - Love 'Em!

Capitalism Communism And Cowism - A New Economics For The 21st Century

Noble Cow - Munching Grass, Looking Curious And Just Hanging Around

Let's Be Friends - A Curious, Calm Cow

Wondrous Glories of Vraja

We Feel Just Like You Do

Tsunami of Diseases Headed Our Way - Know Your Food Before Time Runs Out

Cow Killing And Beef Export - The Master Plan To Turn India Into A Desert By 2050

(More information on availability : DrDasa.com)

Contents

Preface

We have to understand we are not the only beings on this planet with personalities and minds', says Jane Goodall. That makes sense. Even a child knows that. All creatures have a personality and this holds true even for trees and plants what to speak of insects, reptiles, birds and beasts. Any child can attest to this simple fact but modern scientists and religionists often think otherwise.

It was recently reported that European scientists have 'discovered' that domesticated pets can experience something much akin to the human emotions including envy. They have just now got around to studying the human like emotions in pets after having long discounted the experiences and anecdotes of pet owners as anthropomorphizing. For many years, physicians and scientists assumed that other mammals do not experience pain in any significant way.

But does it take a scientist to understand this simple fact that all creatures in this world are sentient? This is known even to a puny animal! How far the human society has degraded can be judged from this fact.

Religionists are not too far behind these dull-headed and stone-hearted 'scientific' claims. In some of the world's prominent religions, animals are denied feelings due to their not possessing a soul. Previously the same folks denied a soul to Red Indians, slaves, Africans and women.

Animals very much possess a soul, a far better one than these soulless religionists do. These so-called religious followers are the ones without a soul.

It is height of arrogance to assume that animals do not have advanced mental and emotional capabilities and deserve some consideration, just because we eat, drink and sleep in some what polished ways.

Because of such widespread misconceptions and mischief, modern man is so soulless in dealing with non-human creatures. He has created a hell on Earth for animals. An advanced country like USA slaughters over one million animals per hour in spite of the easy availability of grains, vegetables and milk to feed everyone.

This book deals with the internal lives of the cows. Cow is a very sober animal and does not wag her tail as often as a dog. This does not mean dog is good and cow is food. All animals including dog should be shown love and care. But cow especially has a serious significance for human existence in this world. Our earlier books on this subject (cowism.com) shed some light on it.

Talk about cows' feelings is often brushed off as fluffy and sentimental but this book would prove it otherwise.

Dr Sahadeva dasa
1st December 2009
Secunderabad, India

1.

The Old Man And The Cow

The Story of An Extraordinary Friendship

What follows is a Story of Ken Simmons from New Zealand, aged 85 and his pet cow "Silverside", aged 38.

Ken Simmons starts cycling around 8am with a homemade backpack lying limp upon his back. He pops in to a couple of properties on the way, collecting scraps of straw to fill his bag. About 30 minutes and three kilometers later, he stops and looks out across the fields. There she is.

The 38-year-old cow has two twisted horns, pale-grey shoulders and a wrinkled neck, a leaking udder and milk running down her ankle.

He named her Silverside, but he only ever calls her Girl.

She was the first cow he bought when he retired. That was 15 years ago. After that, he gradually downscaled his small herd of cows till it numbered just one. And around her he has built a devoted routine; daily rituals that reveal an

elderly man's enjoyment in the simplest of tasks. This is the story of an extraordinary friendship between man and beast, both nearing the end of their long lives.

Every morning, Mr Simmons – "just cracking a young 85" –leaves his bike by a railing and walks across the fields to reach his girl. "Hello, my darling. Hey Bub. Where's my Girl, eh? Where's my Girl?"

He produces a small red apple and she sniffs it out, swallowing it with her furry lips and biting with her last remaining teeth. She has no front teeth. He has just one.

He places straw in her trough, rinses out her bucket of molasses, and lets her out the gate.

"C'mon, Bub." She shuffles off ahead, as he talks about her diet. Every morning, he fills the bucket with two capfuls of trace minerals and a generous slurp of molasses. Her tail lifts and a stream of steaming brown liquid trails to the ground. "Perhaps a little too much molasses," he says, wryly.

It's seven years since Girl had a calf, but one day three years ago she started lactating and hasn't stopped since. Mr Simmons sits on an upturned bucket and drags his fingers over her teats. He checks for signs of mastitis then directs the flow into a jar. He uses the milk to make custard and scones. "That gives her a purpose in life. She thinks she's doing something for me."

38 And Still Going Strong

Yes! This cow has crossed her 38th birthday and since last seven years hasn't calved but still gives milk, probably out of her love for Mr Simmons.

Jenny Weston, senior lecturer in cattle health at Massey University has never heard of a cow making it into its 30s. The average cow lives to seven years. A good milking cow might live to 13 before being culled for failing to get in calf. The oldest recorded cow, according to a cow factoid website, was Big Bertha. She died in 1993, aged 48, having produced 39 calves.

Dr Weston says that a largely toothless cow like Girl would not survive without Mr Simmons. She would starve without hand-feeding as her gums could not rip enough grass.

Love Is Keeping Them Alive

Dr Weston says cows are sociable and, in the absence of other cows, Mr Simmons's companionship is undoubtedly keeping Girl alive.

And maybe vice versa.

He tries not to think about arriving at the farm one day to find his old friend passed away. And if he goes first, she'll be put down. "There wouldn't be anyone who would look after her like I do."

Mr Simmons says she is a good pal, who has never kicked him or used her considerable 350-kilogram bulk to nudge him out of the way. Occasionally, accidentally, she'll stand on his foot, but she would never willingly hurt him.

His Life Revolves Around His Beloved

He wears blue overalls, a woolly jersey, gumboots and a reflector jacket that a friend's wife bought for him. At the roadside, he leans over to hand-feed her little nuts of meal. He suspects the pampering may be the secret to her longevity.

When she's finished eating, she wanders over to the gate that leads on to the road. He watches out as she crosses the tar seal. She can't run anymore and cars tear along the back roads at lethal speeds. "She's not so steady on her feet. Neither am I."

Girl enjoys her walk, grazing on the roadside grass. He watches her every move, taking delight in the changes in her mood. "Oh look, she's puckering her lips." When they get tired, they stop and collapse into the grass.

When bitter winds howl down from the Tararua Ranges, she shelters behind some trees. In the icy heart of winter, when the grass is some days fat with frost and other days sodden by rain, he

dons wet-weather gear and appears at the gate, on cue, to feed her, milk her, walk her. On searingly hot spring days like this, she seeks out cosy hollowed pits on the roadside. "She'll may be meditate, do a bit of grazing . . . I sit down."

Girl lets him know when it's time to go home, usually around 1PM. He walks behind, occasionally lifting her tail and giving it a light tug. "That's the accelerator pedal."

He walks her to her field, and sidles up for a cuddle. "Come to Dad." He gives her a hug, slaps her rump and tells her he'll be back tomorrow.

He packs away her feed, secures his backpack on his back, climbs on his bike and turns to cycle home . . . . back to his pensioner flat and the documentary channel.

Some days he brings a radio, but today, the only sounds are lambs crying and calves blowing hot breath out their noses. After a while, she starts to call out for a cuddle and he duly wanders over and scratches her scrawny, sun-bleached back. "She loves this." Her head tips slightly to the side in obvious pleasure as he rakes his swollen fingers up and down her spine. Often, she'll lick his face in appreciation. "She likes to get into my hair but she just about tears your scalp off."

He spends about five hours a day with his Girl, the rest of it feeding his mind and soul. Mr Simmons was born in Hamilton in 1922, one of four children. His father was a motor engineer. He worked in a dairy factory in Waharoa, in the Waikato, before leaving for World War II. He was a radio operator with the New Zealand Division from 1943 to 1945. His wife separated long ago and his four children live around New Zealand but he doesn't see much of them, his family, his life is his 'Girl'.

Girl is so loved around the town near where they live, she gets more boxes of chocolates for Christmas than he does. "She's an icon." He spends around $200 out of his $500 fortnightly pension payment on her. "She costs me around about $400 a month, so I gotta watch every penny I get."

He pays $10 a week rent on the quarter- acre where Girl sleeps. She is tested for tuberculosis every year. He has bought her a thermal cover for winter and she has all the best supplements on the bovine market.

Mr Simmons looks back on 85 years of memories and says life goes by very quickly. "You blink your bloody eyes and it's gone." His advice is to start praying that you'll come back as a cow; the centre of the world for "some old fellow like me".

©The Dominion Post, NZ

Why should you kill these innocent animals? You take. You keep them muda, happy, and you get so much milk that it will moist, it will make the ground wet. This is civilization. This is civilization.
~Srila Prabhupada (Srimad Bhagavatam, 1.10.4, London, November 25, 1973)

2.

A Mean Leopard

Moo-ved By The Love of A Cow

This is the story of a fearless and affable cow from a village in Gujarat, India. This Story was published by Press Trust of India (PTI), on May 13, 2003.

It was a rare case of predator-prey friendship. A leopard coming to 'visit' a cow at night literally became the talk of the town. The incredible ways of the two animals at Antoli village in Vadodara district attracted the attention of one and all, including the wild life activists.

Local villagers were first to notice the frequent visits of a leopard to the sugarcane field for its close encounter with a cow in the field. Immediately they alerted the wildlife department.

One team comprising wildlife warden Mr Rohit Vyas, conservator of forest H S Singh and other enthusiasts including wildlifer Manoj Thakkar and Kartik Upadhyay visited the village several times for verification and found that the leopard has been visiting the cow from October last year at regular intervals.

Mr Vyas says, "It was unbelievable, they approached each other at very close proximity and the fearless cow licked the leopard on its head and neck. The dogs would bark when the leopard came to meet the waiting cow every night between 9.30 PM to 10.30 PM".

The Forest Department which was trying to capture the beast, gave up its efforts after learning about the friendship. Moreover, the leopard did not harm other animals or human beings in the area. Its visit benefited villagers as other animals who damage the crops were scared away. That year the village's crop yields went up by 30 percent.

> *I am staggered by the colossal arrogance of the majority of the public who regard animals as no more important than table legs. It is also one of the things that has driven me away from Christian religion, as the idea that there is a magic dividing line that allows humans to go to heaven and animals not is no more intelligent than their previous assertion that the world is flat.*
> *~Nick, Cheshire*

> *When you are in the jungle, you are a tiger, you can eat animals. But when you are civilized, when you can produce nice foodstuff, so many nice grains, fruits, and milk, why should you eat meat? That means you are misusing your advanced intelligence improperly. Therefore you must suffer.*
> *~Srila Prabhupada (Lecture on Srimad Bhagavatam, Los Angeles, December 16, 1973)*

3.

Ways To Cool Down An Angry Bull

It was a morning as usual and life was going on like any other day in the city of Changsha, capital of Hunan province in China. In a busy district of the city, a bull was roped to a tree near the road.

Suddenly something transpired and bull became furious and broke loose, grounding the tree to which it was tied. It started attacking the vehicles passing by and created a ruckus.

The police quickly arrived on the scene but had no clue on how to control the situation.

The bull's opera went on for some time and police joined the crowd of hapless onlookers.

Amidst the crowd of onlookers was a farmer who had a better idea. He ran to his yard nearby and hurried to the spot with a cow.

Surprisingly, the bull calmed down and walked off the scene with the cow.

4.

Looking Beyond Their Exterior

When you see cows standing in the pasture blandly chewing some dreary bit of grass and staring into the middle distance, you'd never guess what lies beneath that placid exterior.

A cow contentedly chewing her cud may look like she doesn't have a care in the world, but there's a lot going on behind those big brown eyes. Cows are as diverse as cats, dogs, and people: Some are bright; others are slow learners. Some are bold and adventurous; others are shy and timid. Some are friendly and considerate; others are bossy and devious. According to organic farmer Rosamund Young, author of *The Secret Lives of Cows*, cows "can be highly intelligent, moderately so, or slow to understand; friendly, considerate, aggressive, docile, inventive, dull, proud, or shy."

According to recent research, in addition to having distinct personalities, cows are generally very intelligent animals who can remember things for a long time. Animal behaviorists have found that cows interact in socially complex ways, developing friendships over time, sometimes holding grudges against cows or man who treat them badly, forming social hierarchies within their herds, and choosing leaders based upon intelligence. They are emotionally complex as well and even have the capacity to worry about the future.

For meat eaters, once they were a byword for mindless docility. But modern research is finding out that cows have a complex mental life. Of course, even a child in traditional cultures knew this all along.

Like all other living beings, cows are capable of strong emotions such as pain, fear and even anxiety about the future. But if farmers provide the right conditions, they can also feel great happiness.

They are reconsidering the welfare laws because they are finding cows so emotionally similar to humans

Christine Nicol, professor of animal welfare at Britain's Bristol University, says even chickens might have to be treated as individuals with needs and problems. She says, "Remarkable cognitive abilities and cultural innovations have been revealed. Our challenge is to teach others that every animal we intend to eat or use is a complex individual, and to adjust our farming culture accordingly."

Her colleague John Webster adds: "People have assumed intelligence is linked to the ability to suffer, and that because animals have smaller brains they suffer less than humans. That is a pathetic piece of logic."

The Bristol researchers have documented how cows within a herd form friendship groups of between two and four animals with whom

they spend most of their time, often grooming and licking each other. They will also dislike other cows, and can bear grudges for months or years.

The assumption that farm animals cannot suffer from conditions that would be intolerable for humans is partly based on the idea they have no sense of self. Latest research refutes this nonsensical idea. Sentient animals have the capacity to experience pleasure and are motivated to seek it.

Prof. Webster adds, "You only have to watch how cows and lambs both seek and enjoy pleasure when they lie with their heads raised to the sun on a perfect English summer's day. Just like humans."

This is very essential to keep cows very comfortably. If they feel comfortable, then you get the most nourishing food, milk. We are practically seeing in our New Vrindaban center, because the cow are feeling secure in our custody, they're delivering milk up to the eighty pounds daily. You'll be surprised.
~Srila Prabhupada (Lecture, Srimad-Bhagavatam 1.16.19,
Hawaii, January 15, 1974)

5.

Motherly Licks That Saved A Life

Dr. Ravi Kolhe is a kind hearted doctor who has been providing medical care to local tribals in Melghat region of Maharashtra, India, for the last 25 years. Due to his selfless service, child mortality rate in that area has come down from 200 to 60 out of 1000.

Years ago, one day in the late evening, he saw an old man taking a cow somewhere. Curious, he inquired as to where the man was going with his cow so late in the evening. Initially hesitant, the old man said the cow was a 'bhakad' (Marathi word for a dry, old cow) and he was going to sell it to a butcher. (In India cows are considered sacred and hence the hesitancy.)

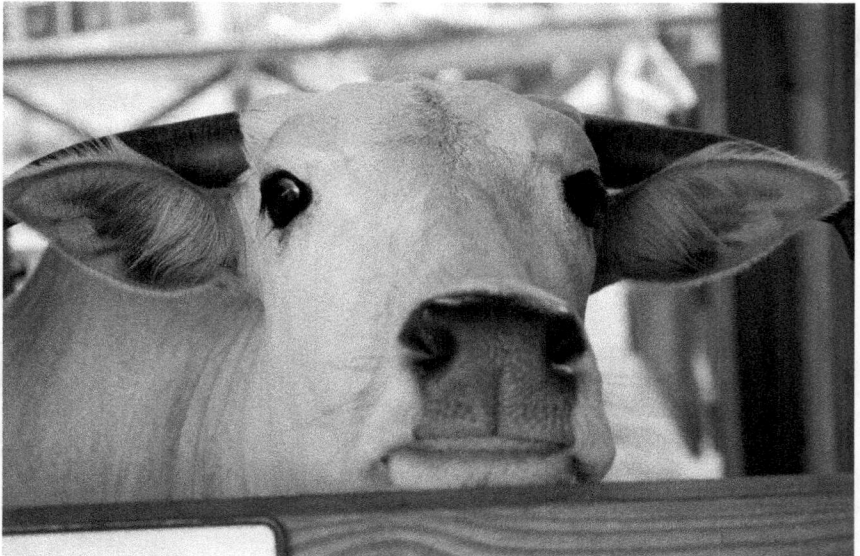

Taking compassion, Dr Kolhe asked the man to tie the cow in his frontyard and offered him Rs.200 which was way more than the man expected for his cow. Doctor and his family members started taking care of the cow.

Doctor's wife happened to be carrying at the time. After few days, at the time of delivery several complications arose. A stillborn baby was delivered and the mother's condition turned serious.

The doctor hastily placed the 'dead' baby in the front yard and rushed back to peform a post delivery operation to save his wife's life.

In the meantime, the cow in the front yard broke free and approached the baby and started licking him all over. This went on for sometime. After a while the doctor heard the child crying. Shocked, the doctor rushed to the yard and picked the baby up. Gradually his wife also recovered.

Now the boy is around 20 years old and studying for his engineering degree.

This is a real incident. Dr Kolhe or his son can be reached at the following address:

Dr. Ravi Kolhe
Kolupur Melghat,
(Paratwada-Indore way) Taluk: Dharni
Dist: Amaravati, Maharashtra, India
Ph: 07226-202002, 07227-202829; 202692

Now, mother, your cow is your mother. You drink milk of cow. And the bull is your father. Because without bull, without the cow and bull being united, there is no milk. So how is that you are eating your father and mother? It is a great challenge. Actually those who are meat-eater, beef-eater, they are killing their father and mother and become implicated in sinful life.
~*Srila Prabhupada (Lecture, Srimad Bhagavatam 1.16.3, Los Angeles, December 31, 1973)*

21

6.

Brainy Bovines

Researchers have found that cows can not only figure out problems, they also, like humans, enjoy the intellectual challenge and get excited when they find a solution. Their big problem, of course, is that they're being raised for slaughter, and just like all animals, they don't want to be separated from their families, and they don't want to die. So cows have been known to use their smarts to perform amazing feats, such as leaping over a six-foot fence to escape from a slaughterhouse, walking seven miles to reunite with a calf after being sold at auction, and swimming across a river to freedom.

Cows are intelligent and curious animals who enjoy solving problems and interacting with their environment. They have long memories and are capable of learning lessons from each other, just as humans do

Cows like challenges, and according to researchers, they feel excitement when they finish a task or use their intellect to overcome an obstacle. Donald Broom, professor of animal welfare at Cambridge University, has researched on cow intelligence and found that cows can become

excited by solving intellectual challenges. In one study, researchers challenged the animals with a task where they had to find how to open a door to get some food. An electroencephalograph was used to measure their brainwaves. The brainwaves showed their excitement; their heartbeat went up and some even jumped into the air. "We called it their Eureka moment," says Professor Broom.

Research has further shown that cows clearly understand cause-and-effect relationships—a sure-fire sign of advanced cognitive abilities. For example, cows can learn how to push a lever to operate a drinking fountain when they're thirsty or to press a button with their heads to release grain when they're hungry. Like humans and other animals, cows also quickly learn to stay away from things that cause them pain, like electric fences and unkind humans.

Because of their complex social interactions, cows also have the ability to learn from each other, another indication of their advanced intelligence. According the Humane Society of the United States, if an individual cow in a herd is shocked by an electric fence, the rest will become alarmed and learn to avoid it. Only a small fraction will ever be shocked.

"Why injustice? These poor animals, they are also my subject. How you can kill them? He's also born in this land." "National" means one is born in that particular land. So they are also born in this land. Why he should be treated differently? Just like in your country, even one Indian gets his child here, the child is counted as USA-born, US citizen, eh? Immediately. So if that is the law, that anyone born in this land should be treated as national, what is this law that the cows and the bulls born in that land, they are to be slaughtered? What is this law?*
~Srila Prabhupada (Lecture, Srimad-Bhagavatam 1.16.4, Los Angeles, January 1, 1974)*

7.

Cows Don't Want to Die

Like all animals, cows value their lives and don't want to die. Stories abound of cows who have gone to extraordinary lengths to fight for their lives.

A cow named Suzie was about to be loaded on a freighter bound for Venezuela when she turned around, ran back down the gangplank, and leaped into the river. Even though she was pregnant, she managed to swim all the way across the river, eluding capture for several days. She was rescued by PETA and sent to a sanctuary for farmed animals.

When workers at a slaughterhouse in Massachusetts went on break, Emily the cow made a break of her own. She took a tremendous leap over a five-foot gate and escaped into the woods,

surviving for several weeks in New England's snowiest winter in a decade, cleverly refusing to touch the hay put out to lure her back to the slaughterhouse. When she was eventually caught by the owners of a nearby sanctuary, public outcry demanded that the slaughterhouse allow the sanctuary to buy her for one dollar. Today, Emily is living happily in Massachusetts, a testimony to the fact that eating meat means eating animals who don't want to die. (Emily's full story will be related in next chapter.)

> All my life I have loved cows and everything about them. And I think killing them for their skin and meat should be stopped. Cows are not there for fashion.
> ~Shayda Ansar

Much like humans, cows vary widely in intelligence and personality. Some seem bold and adventurous while others are shy and reserved. Some cows are very clever but some learn slowly. They can be friendly or aggressive, and sometimes even appear to be proud.

> you are ungrateful. You are drinking milk, you are taking so much butter, milk product, and as gratitude you are killing cows? You should be ashamed. Even if you have no human feelings. You suck the breast of your mother and kill? Is that humanity?
> ~Srila Prabhupada (Lecture, Bhagavad-gita 3.11-19, Los Angeles, December 27, 1968)

8.

Emily the Cow Who Saved Herself

Emily knew that danger was near. She had never been in a place like this before—a little shed with a five-foot gate behind her. All of her companions had gone through the swinging doors in front of her, and not one had returned. The men who had locked the gate at Frank Arena's slaughterhouse in Hopkinton, Mass., were now off having lunch. Emily saw her chance, and she took it.

When she made her move, jaws dropped and workers stared in amazement. Suddenly, Emily—all 1,600 pounds of her was airborne, sailing over the gate and out of the building. "A cow just can't do that," exclaimed a butcher.

As residents of this rural area west of Boston were to discover, Emily, a three-year-old Holstein, can do many things cows aren't supposed to do.

Slaughterhouse workers took off after their runaway animal, but she disappeared into the woods and eluded them all day. It was November, 1995, the beginning of an odyssey that would capture the imagination of the entire community. They scoured the woods, leaving out bales of hay to entice Emily back into their grasp. She would have none of it.

Some years ago an English woman who had the gift of being able to understand animals came to my shelter in Delhi. Walking up to a cow, she turned to me and said " She says that her head still hurts " The woman did not know that the cow had been in an accident.
~Maneka Gandhi

26

Instead, people reported seeing her running with a herd of deer, learning from them how to forage in the woods. Soon the local paper was running updates on Emily sightings.

Some residents began to think, "There's got to be some way we can purchase her and let her live in peace." Soon it seemed that nobody wanted to see her captured. Local farmers started leaving out bales of hay for her to eat.

When the residents contacted the slaughterhouse owners, they were touched by their willingness to help. Granddaughter of the slaughterhouse owner, Angela, had given Emily her name, and even Frank (the owner) seemed impressed by her pluck. At first he offered to let the residents have Emily for the bargain price of $350; then, after consulting his granddaughter, he changed the price to $1.

A blizzard hit, and Emily's food sources were covered by snow. Local farmers brought grain, hay, and water to places where they thought Emily might be found; the food was eaten after they left, but Emily wasn't ready to reveal herself.

Finally, one December day after they spread out some food, the

residents saw Emily. "We looked over our shoulder, and she was right there looking at us," one of them recalls. Emily had lost 500 pounds and needed veterinary treatment after her 40-day ordeal, but the loving care of her well-wishers brought her back to her full weight.

Emily became a celebrity in the community and people looked after her well. Soon she had a company. Gabriel, a calf that was rescued on his way to a local slaughterhouse and put in the shelter along with Emily. Emily groomed and licked him as fastidiously as any loving mom. Further she was joined by a pair of turkeys, a mother goat and her two kids, and three rabbits—all of them rescued from inhumane conditions.

But Emily's biggest test was yet to come. Ellen Little, producer of 1995's film Richard III, started work on a film version of Emily's saga. Emily did not have to leave her happy home for the lights of Hollywood, though. She was played by another Holstein—and that gave another cow a chance to become a star. (By Michael Ryan, Parade Magazine, May 4, 1997)

These are just a few of the countless stories of cows who value their lives and fear death, just like humans and all other animals. In the world., more than 75 million cows are killed in the meat and dairy industries every year. When they are still very young, cows are burned with hot irons (branding), their testicles are ripped out of their scrotums (castration), and their horns are cut or burned off—

Cows, however, are never meant to be killed or eaten by human beings. In every sastra, cow killing is vehemently condemned. Indeed, one who kills a cow must suffer for as many years as there are hairs on the body of a cow. Manu-samhita says, pravrttir esa bhutanam nivrttis tu maha-phala: we have many tendencies in this material world, but in human life one is meant to learn how to curb those tendencies. Those who desire to eat meat may satisfy the demands of their tongues by eating lower animals, but they should never kill cows, who are actually accepted as the mothers of human society because they supply milk.
~Srila Prabhupada (Srimad Bhagavatam 6.4.9)

all without painkillers. Once they have grown big enough, they are sent to massive, muddy feedlots to be fattened for slaughter.

Millions of cows living on dairy farms spend most of their lives either in large sheds or on feces-caked mud lots where disease is rampant. Cows raised for their milk are repeatedly impregnated, and their calves are taken from them and sent to veal farms or other dairy farms. When their exhausted bodies can no longer produce enough milk, they are sent to slaughter and ground up for hamburgers.

Many cows die on the way to slaughter, and those who survive are shot in the head with a bolt gun, hung up by their legs, and taken onto the killing floor, where their throats are cut and they are skinned. Some cows remain fully conscious throughout the entire process—according to one slaughterhouse worker, in an interview with the *Washington Post*, "they die piece by piece."

Animals too have a right to live.....just like we do. They were created just like we were. Why people kill them for food? I believe a lot in Karma....I'm sure people who treat animals with cruelty are going to be reborn as animals, with the same cruelty meted out to them. An animal, unless fierce and wild, would never kill humans for food. They always reciprocate the love and kindness we shower them with. But look at what we humans do to them, in spite of being knowledgable and aware. May God enlighten such people.
~Donald Perez, Portland

Also keep in mind that every time you choose to buy a leather jacket or leather shoes, you sentence animals to a lifetime of suffering. Buying leather directly contributes to factory farms and slaughterhouses, since the skins of animals are the most economically important by-product of the multibillion-dollar meat industry.

You can help these gentle, intelligent, sensitive animals by removing their flesh from your diet and refusing to wear their skins. To get started, get your *free vegetarian starter kit*, packed with nutrition information, shopping tips, delicious recipes, and much more from the many sites that are selling them on internet. There are thousands of websites on vegetarianism, animal cruelty etc. which can be referred to. One out of many such sites is VegCooking.com which offers cruelty-free recipes, vegetarian products, cookbook recommendations, and a shopping guide. Kurma dasa and Yamuna devi dasi are some of the world renowned chefs whose vegetarian cooking books have sold by millions. Higher Taste (available at krishna.com) is another great book which offers mouthwatering vegetarian recipes and irrefutable arguments for a vegetarian lifestyle.

What is the purpose of eating? To live. If you can live very peacefully, very nicely, with good health, by eating so many varieties of foodstuff given by Krishna, why should I kill an animal? This is humanity. Why should I imitate an animal? Then what is the difference between animal and human being? If you have no discretion, if you have no consciousness.

Besides that, scientifically, your teeth is meant for eating vegetables. The tiger has teeth for eating meat. Nature has made it like that. It has to kill another... Therefore he has got nails, he has got teeth, he has got strength. But you have no such strength. You cannot kill a cow like that, pouncing like tiger. You have to make slaughterhouse and sit down at your home. Somebody may slaughter, and you can eat very nicely. What is this? You do like tiger. Pounce upon a cow and eat.

~Srila Prabhupada (Bhagavad-gita 3.11-19 — Los Angeles, December 27, 1968)

9.

Cows Never Forget a Place or a Face

Cows don't forget lessons that they've learned. Research has shown that these animals have impressive memories. Cows remember their homes and can find their way back to their favorite spots.

According to one report on cow behavior, cows "demonstrate good spatial memory and they remember where things are located. They can remember migration routes, watering holes, shelter and the location of their newborn calf." Researchers also report that cows can remember the best eating spots in a pasture and that they use their spatial memory to guide themselves back to the best spots.

Stories of cows who used their navigation capabilities to find their way back home after being sold at auction are common. Some cows never forget those who have hurt them either, and they've been known to hold grudges against other members of their herd. Author, Rosamund Young, details a quarrel between a grandmother cow and her daughter. Grandmother cows often help their daughters with mothering duties, but a cow named Olivia wanted no part of that. She never left her calf's side, and she ignored her mother's offers to help groom him. Offended, her mother finally marched off to another field to graze with her friends and never "spoke" to her daughter again. Cows can also remember and hold grudges against people who have hurt them or their family members.

> *I Love cows too, I live in a Finnish cattle farm, we have altogether about 50 cows and calfs. And who said all the cows look the same? I remember our every cow's name! All cows have their own personality - someone is small, someone is big, someone is very friendly, someone is a bit careful, someone likes patting their head, someone likes grooming... But they all are so lovely - I can't get enough of watching their big, friendly eyes or when they are eating the grass outside.*
> *~Kenneth, Finland.*

> *The productive class, they should give protection to the cows. The cows are given under their protection, not that "Because the cows are given under my protection, therefore I must open a slaughterhouse and kill them." Similarly... So children under the protection of father and mother... Just like this child is sitting on the lap of... He is comfortable. But if the father thinks, "He is under my protection; therefore I shall cut throat..." Now it is going on. The abortion means that. The child is taken shelter of the mother's womb for protection, but now she is being killed. The time is so bad.*
> *~Srila Prabhupada (Lecture, Srimad Bhagavatam 1.15.34, Los Angeles, December 12, 1973)*

10.
Wooden Cow Moo-ves Hearts

What to speak of a real cow, a wooden cow cutout has stirred the feelings of a town in mid-west US.

Ms Collins set up two life-size wooden cow cutouts on the range across the street from her home on Roxbury Road. After few days, one of the two wooden cutouts was stolen during the weekend. So Collins hand-painted a sign made out of plywood that said, "Please bring my sister back, I miss her. Thanks, Bessie."

A few days later, the cow cutout remarkably reappeared.

Collins, you could say, was moo-ved.

"Somebody felt so bad after seeing the sign that they were so kind to return it," Collins said. "So many times you hear about the people in this world, but there are still some honest people out there."

So another sign went up next to the 3-foot-tall cows: "Thanks for bringing my sister back. Thanks, Bessie."

Since the incident, Collins said her phone has been ringing

constantly from people calling to ask about what happened with the cows. People driving by have been slowing down to read the sign.

"I thought, 'It's just a wooden cow.' I didn't think it would mean so much to people," Collins says.

I love cows, they are so special creatures. I think they are more closely related to us then apes. They have the same characteristics as we do. there is nothing better then to sit and watch cows in the field, eating, playing, scraping. Hopefully they inherit the planet when were gone.
~Jeff Young, Long Beach

Always Curious

11.

The Social Lives of Cows

A herd of cows has a complex social dynamics. Each cow can recognize more than 100 members of the herd, and social relationships are very important to them. Cows will consistently choose leaders for their intelligence, inquisitiveness, confidence, experience, and good social skills, while bullying, selfishness, size, and strength are not recognized as suitable leadership qualities. Cows form close friendships with some members of their herd—the relationships between mothers and daughters are especially strong, and calves bond with others in their peer group.

Researchers at Bristol University in the United Kingdom found that cows have best friends and cliques, just like human beings do, and that animals groom and lick one another to demonstrate this

affection. The longer partners know each other, the longer they groom each other. Also like humans, cows may carefully avoid others in their herd after they've had a falling out.

The social relationships between cows influence many parts of their daily lives. For example, when the herd settles down for a nap, each cow's position and the order in which they lie down is directly related to their status in the herd.

Raising cows in unnatural conditions, such as crowded feedlots, is very stressful to them because it upsets their hierarchy. University of Saskatchewan researcher Jon Watts notes that cows who are kept in groups of more than 200 on commercial feedlots get stressed and constantly fight for dominance (feedlots in America hold thousands of cows at a time). He says that this occurs because the cows are taken from their mothers too early, deprived of adequate space, and can't find their niche within such large groups.

We have three cows... Brisket, Burgy and T-bone. Our cows are as gentle as puppy dogs. Burgy is a really smart cow and knows how to open the bag of pellets. He also knows how to pick up a bucket by the handle!
~Deborah Lee, Wisconsin

This is akin to how humans would feel if we were penned in a tiny space with thousands of unfamiliar people. Just like us, cows like to be near their families and friends, and the stress of life on factory farms makes them feel confused, scared, and alone.

The cow is the most important animal for developing the human body to perfection. The body can be maintained by any kind of foodstuff, but cow's milk is particularly essential for developing the finer tissues of the human brain so that one can understand the intricacies of transcendental knowledge. A civilized man is expected to live on foodstuffs comprising fruits, vegetables, grains, sugar and milk. The bull helps in the agricultural process of producing grain, etc., and thus in one sense the bull is the father of humankind, whereas the cow is the mother, for she supplies milk to human society. A civilized man is therefore expected to give all protection to the bulls and cows.
~Srila Prabhupada (Srimad Bhagavatam 3.5.7)

12.

Canada Owes A Lot To This Cow

The war of 1812 between Britain, (including Canadians), and the U.S. was to determine the scope of each one's control. The Americans were intent on pushing into Canada. One lady, Laura Secord was loyal to Britain and lived with her husband James, in the small village of Queenston, in what was then Upper Canada, now the province of Ontario.

One June 21, 1813, a group of American soldiers took over their home. James, her husband, was recovering from wounds he'd suffered at one of the Battle six months previously. Laura gave the soldier food and drink. Quite a lot of drink. Stimulated by alcohol the soldiers talked openly about a plan to surprise British Lt. Fitzgibbon (local commander at that time), destroy his headquarters, take the British and Canadian soldiers prisoners and occupy the Niagara Peninsula.

When Laura Secord heard this, she was alarmed. She decided to warn the local commanding officer Lt. Fitzgibbon. But how? Her husband James Secord could barely walk.

Laura decided to go herself. It was a long 20 miles trek to Beaver Dams where Lt. Fitzgibbon was posted. And she had to have a good reason to go in that wilderness, otherwise it will raise the suspicion of American sentries because women at that time hardly left their homes.

Wisely, Laura came up with an idea. When she left her home, at dawn on June 22, she'd also taken her cow, as a cover for her mission. Enemy soldiers patrolling the area might accept her tale of taking the cow to another farm for which there were any number of logical reasons. Sentries, probably country boys themselves, would likely believe her.

Laura and the cow continued. It was a daunting journey. The twenty mile trek from Queenston to Beaver Dams took her along country roads, across meadows, into thick woods and through stagnant swamps.

Wolves, wildcats and snakes inhabited the country.

Lt. Fitzgibbon never forgot that day. "The weather of the 22nd of June 1813 was very hot and Mrs. Secord, whose person was slight and delicate, appeared to have been, and no doubt was, very much exhausted by the exertion she made in coming to me.", he wrote in 1827.

Laura and her cow began their trek at dawn. It was dark when she left the final swamp, climbed a rocky escarpment, pushed through heavy underbrush and encountered Indians loyal to the British. They escorted Laura and the cow to Lt. Fitzgibbon. Consequently all but six of the American soldiers were captured, the garrison was safe and Niagara stayed Canadian.

In 1813 women generally stayed close to their house and hearth. The cow gave Laura a good excuse for being so far from home. Since James Secord couldn't walk, if the cow had to be taken somewhere, well who but Laura would take her? And Laura knew she needed a good excuse. Spies, if caught, were executed by firing squad. Getting the cow through swamp and forest might have been difficult, but it was preferable to being caught and shot. A woman determined to risk her life to warn the British of an American assault was certainly clever enough to provide herself with an alibi.

The sturdy cow was a familiar comfort and support, staying firmly by her mistress' side. Never once mooing, "It's too hot and the bugs are terrible. Can we go back now?" Canada owes a lot to that cow.

Most Canadians know of Laura Secord and her cow.

> Cows are such gentle natured and each have different personalities. They are very genuine and so kind. We human should learn from them!
> I hate (and do not understand) how the insult 'you're a cow' came about, as these creatures are anything but humans at their worst! I love them. They need to be recognized as more than meat.
> ~Steven Green, Seattle

> The cow is the mother because just as one sucks the breast of one's mother, human society takes cow's milk. Similarly, the bull is the father of human society because the father earns for the children just as the bull tills the ground to produce food grains. Human society will kill its spirit of life by killing the father and the mother.
> ~Srila Prabhupada (Srimad Bhagavatam 3.2.29)

13.

Gentle Giants

Cows are emotional animals who have likes and dislikes, just like humans do. The chairman of the National Farmers Union in the United Kingdom, Tim Sell, explains, "They are all individuals and all have their own characteristics. They are tremendously curious. They have emotional storms. When it is a miserable, cold day, they will all be miserable, but when it is nice and sunny, you can almost see them smiling."

Many cows are affectionate animals who are deeply loyal to their families and human companions. Cows can use their body posture and vocal sounds to express a whole range of emotions, including contentment, interest, anger, and distress. These gentle giants mourn the death of those they love, even shedding tears over their loss.

Like humans and all animals, cows show strong reactions to bad treatment. For example, Dr. Ed Pajor of Purdue University found that cows resent being handled roughly: "The handlers don't have to be really mean and hit the cows. It's just a slap on the rump in the way that many farmers would. But the cows don't like it and it makes a real difference."

With kind treatment, cows can be very loyal companions. Anyone who has spent time with cows knows that they look out for their friends, both human and animal. In her book *Peaceful Kingdom: Random Acts of Kindness by Animals*, Stephanie Laland writes that when the Rev. O. F. Robertson began to go blind, his cow Mary became his "seeing-eye cow." Mary would walk along with him, nudging him away from obstacles. She diligently accompanied Robertson everywhere he went for the rest of his life.

Why I love cows?
Why I love cows? Well, I rent a piece of land opposite a meadow where the farmer has two cows. Each year (regrettably) the eldest is destined for meat... In the meantime (mean time for the animals), I try to make their limited life-span as comfortable as possible by offering them carrots. This has been going on for many years and I'm still surprised by the difference in personality structure these animals have: cuddly ones, downright naughty ones, playful or indifferent ones .. a vast variety of character traits that one also finds in humans.
Well, to answer the question why I love them ... they are all individuals and to talk to them, and stare into the deepness of their beautiful eyes gives me a feeling of connection to an animal world that is much closer to us than most people imagine!
~Ray Massart, Belgium

14.

Cows To Reform Prisoners In Indian Jails

Jail authorities in India's Bareilly central jail (Uttar Pradesh) have come up with a novel idea to reform criminals - service to cows! Now prison inmates will have to regularly bathe, feed and milk cows, considered sacred to Hindus.

Senior Jail Superintendent B.R.Verma says "The whole idea behind the plan is inspired by the sacredness of the cow. We all know the cow is revered as a mother by Hindus and has a special mention in holy scriptures that say serving cows cleanses the soul of every sin. Going by the belief that 'go seva' (cow service) leads to salvation, we conceptualized this plan."

In Vedic tradition, the cow is not considered a money-making machine but a sacred animal, an entity who softens human passions, elevating humanity to the mode of goodness so that it can lead a peaceful and harmonious life.

The cow is considered very sacred in Vedic tradition for very good reason. It's good qualities are those that we can emulate.

Serene by temperament, herbivorous by diet, the very appearance of a white cow evokes a sense of piety. Therefore Vedic authorities strictly forbid cow killing.

According to jail officials, nine cows have been brought from Punjab at an estimated cost of Rs.200,000.

This central jail has 3,000 prisoners and most of them are showing enthusiasm in taking care of the cows. The milk from the cows is being given to frail and sick prisoners.

Words alone cannot describe the respect and love I have for cows. I have an experience of how cows have facilitated and bridged reconciliation and unity among communities in my village. And this is one of so many other crucial services cows have and are still serving ......so I say 'Long Live Cows'. ~Innocent Sebasaza Mugisha

Prison authorities are trying to acquire more cows. In the meantime, prisoners are taking turns to do the go-seva. The results are positive and aggressive prisoners seemed to have 'cooled down a bit'.

The Western Way of Prisoner Reform - Cow Killing

Thousands of jails in America, Australia and Europe have in-house slaughterhouses which take care of meat supply to the inmates and even to outside stores.

Jails offer different engagement to its inmates but probably the most sought-after jobs are in the slaughterhouses. These jobs are especially popular with violent offenders. And the most sought-after job of all, which one has to fight for, is the job of the slaughterer himself.

Here we can cite the example of Ohio prison inmates in USA who boast of working in on-site, blood-splattered slaughterhouse, where in about two days a cow is reduced to hamburger patties.

Once the cows have been beheaded, the workers use power saws to split the animals into halves. Farther down the assembly line, they use knives sharp enough to stab through cutting boards to carve meat off the bones of the carcasses.

"It really is a unique environment. If you think about it, we're actually handing the inmates weapons every day," said Warden Jim Erwin of Pickaway Correctional Institution.

Pungent smells and ghastly sights aside, this is highly sought-after work by inmates who must pass a job interview to get the jobs, which pay between 21 cents and $1 an hour.

The knives used in the operation are tethered to the tables. Ronnell Guerry, one of the prisoners boasts, "We take pride in this meat, Some of us might not get along, but we have to put our differences aside and work together." The state has more than 49,000 inmates.

The inmates slaughter almost 500 head of cattle and hogs each week. They make sausages, beef and pork patties, cut beef and pork roasts.

The inmates work behind locked doors. As for those knives: Each is tethered to a table. Other potential weapons, like metal meat hooks, are counted often. Beyond that, the prisoners have to walk through a metal detector to leave the building for the day.

In Ohio, officials are 'proudest' of the efficiency of the meat-processing center, which now doubles as a classroom for a few of the inmates participating in a career center program through Ohio State University's agriculture department.

But the question remains whether violence can reform ones who are already convicted for violent crimes. This training in the 'art of killing' can hardly benefit any one. Once out, they just might kill some one with more ease than before.

No wonder, since 1960, per capita crime rates have more than tripled, while violent crime rates have nearly quintupled all over the world. In an advanced country like US, Department of Justice estimated that 83 percent of all Americans are victims of violent crime at least once in their lives. About a quarter would be victims of three or more violent crimes.

Increasing crime rate means more murders, rapes, robberies, aggravated assaults, burglaries, and auto thefts. At about 50 per 100,000, Washington DC has the highest murder rate in the developed world.

Violence is also increasing among teenagers and other youths. Crime is not a function of poverty but the overall moral fabric of the society. The total number of prisoners in the United States increased from

But it's true if I had to kill them myself I'd be a vegetarian at once. I had to kill a sick wild rabbit once. It was the worst experience of my life. ~Jason Harris

319,000 in 1980 to 1.3 million in 1999. Another 523,000 people were also in jail. This translates into 1 in every 150 Americans being in prison or jail. The present ratio of the population in prison is more than four times what it was in the mid 1970s. Does it have anything to do with flesh diet and rampant slaughterhouse culture?

Which is better, to kill cows or to protect cows, can be gauged from the facts stated above.

When I was living in Austria, and walking in the mountains regularly, I often saw cows noticing, watching, and seemingly 'commenting on' the many hang-gliders, and paragliders, landing in their fields.
-Howard, Dawlish, Devon

15.

Cows Grieve

When they are separated from their families, friends, or human companions, cows grieve over the loss. Researchers report that cows become visibly distressed after even a brief separation. The mother-calf bond is particularly strong, and there are countless reports of mother cows who continue to frantically call and search for their babies after the calves have been taken away and sold to veal farms.

Author Oliver Sacks, M.D., wrote of a visit that he and cattle expert Dr. Temple Grandin made to a dairy farm and of the great tumult of bellowing that they heard when they arrived: "'They must have separated the calves from the cows this morning,' Temple said,

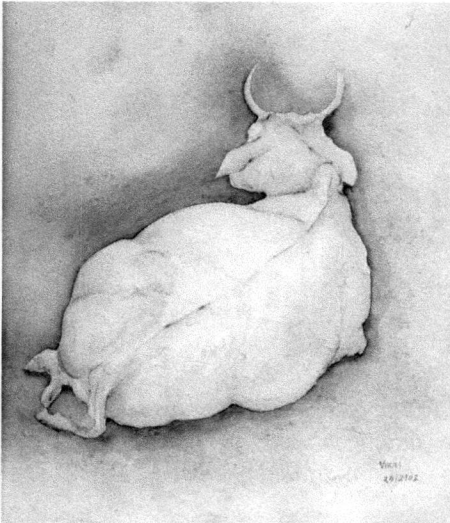

and, indeed, this was what had happened. They saw one cow outside the stockade, roaming, looking for her calf, and bellowing. 'That's not a happy cow,' Temple said. 'That's one sad, unhappy, upset cow. She wants her baby. Bellowing for it, hunting for it. She'll forget for a while, then start again. It's like grieving, mourning—not much written about it. People don't like to allow them thoughts or feelings.'

John Avizienius, the senior scientific officer in the Farm Animal Department of the RSPCA in Britain, says that he "remembers one particular cow who appeared to be deeply affected by the separation from her calf for a period of at least six weeks. When the calf was first removed, she was in acute grief; she stood outside the pen where she had last seen her calf and bellowed for her offspring for hours. She would only move when forced to do so. Even after six weeks, the mother would gaze at the pen where she last saw her calf and sometimes wait momentarily outside of the pen. It was almost as if her spirit had been broken and all she could do was to make token gestures to see if her calf would still be there."

Cows are as ever like humans. They have babies and want to care for their young just as human beings with their babies. So treat cows with respect and we will all feel happy in that environment.
~ Jenny Mc kinney

The vaisyas, the members of the mercantile communities, are especially advised to protect the cows. Cow protection means increasing the milk productions, namely curd and butter. Agriculture and distribution of the foodstuff are the primary duties of the mercantile community backed by education in Vedic knowledge and trained to give in charity. As the ksatriyas were given charge of the protection of the citizens, vaisyas were given the charge of the protection of animals. Animals are never meant to be killed. Killing of animals is a symptom of barbarian society. For a human being, agricultural produce, fruits and milk are sufficient and compatible foodstuffs. The human society should give more attention to animal protection.
~Srila Prabhupada (Srimad Bhagavatam 1.9.26)

16.

She Liked To Listen To Your Story

L uba from Scandinavia reports of an experience from her life which has something to do with her father and a neighbor's cow. Following is her story.

"I know cows have feelings because my Dad had a way with cows. My Dad was a wonderful man but he loved his wine and it did create a lot of unhappiness for the family....But I've witnessed him walking home very intoxicated, with a bottle under his arm, stop at the fence and talk to the neighbor's cow....and she listened. She really looked like she enjoyed the conversation for she never walked away until he himself left to come home....and she would wait for him at the fence whenever he showed up late.

That was one of the funny memories I have of Dad when he was intoxicated....(Luba, June 2005)

The bull and the cow are the symbols of the most offenseless living beings because even the stool and urine of these animals are utilized to benefit human society.
~Srila Prabhupada (Srimad Bhagavatam 1.17.13)

17.

The Brave Russian Bull

G agik Buniatyan, a Russian author, narrates an incident in his famous book "Salted Bread" which deals with persecution of Hare Krishna devotees in Russia during pre-perestroika days.

When Gagik Buniatyan was imprisoned in a Russian Psychiatric hospital (for the crime of believing in God), he and his friends had to deal with a crazy inmate who was a former butcher and was convicted for raping a minor. Usually in a very disturbed condition, one day the former butcher was in somewhat normal condition and narrated an amazing story from his life.

One day while the butcher was working in a slaughterhouse, killing animals with his axe, he happened to see something very unusual which made him scared and astonished.

As usual, they brought one huge bull to the slaughterhouse in a big truck, to be killed by him and his friends. The bull refused to

Of course animals are sentient beings! It is only the desire to maximize profit and fill the supermarket shelves which has led to animals being kept in abysmal concentration-camp style factory farms. Here they lead a bleak short life without natural sunlight, food pumped full of growth hormones and kept in unnatural conditions. The journey to the slaughter house entails further suffering - packed onto lorries, shamelessly squashed together and often, shipped abroad for slaughter in foreign abattoirs where their short lives are ended in barbaric ways...It is human arrogance which has led us to wrongly assume that only we are capable of emotions! Animals love, feel pain, joy, depression like us. What a shame that the meat industry chooses to ignore this fact in the name of profit.
~Yasmin, Birmingham, UK

come out of the truck, even after heavy beating with sticks by the butchers. This butcher felt the bull knew exactly what they were trying to do to him, and so was screaming and trying to hit them with his huge horns. They tried everything they could and bull still didn't move an inch. Then, one of the butchers tied a chain around the bull's neck and the other end to a post next to the entrance. Then the truck was driven forward. So the bull had no other option but to jump down from the truck. He hurt himself badly which made him even angrier.

Somehow they pushed the bull inside the building and brought

him to the third floor where they were supposed to give him an electric shock, kill him and cut him into many pieces. But as soon as they opened the third floor door and pushed the bull in, he started to run around. With his huge horns he was breaking all the machinery and equipments which were used for killing thousands and thousands of innocent animals. Sparks and smoke flew everywhere from the burning electric cables. The metal hooks and equipment fell on the concrete floor, making an overwhelming noise. Everyone was so scared that they locked the iron bar door and just watched the whole scene from there. The bull started to attack them through the door and was trying to smash the iron bars. He seemed ready to kill all of them right there, one by one. As blood was pouring from his horns and body, the bull was screaming from the pain and anger. He started to run around helplessly.

For a moment, the bull stopped in front of the bars, looked straight into the eyes of the butchers, and then turned around and ran towards the window covered with steel bars, he jumped, pushing the whole window out of the wall. He then fell down from the third floor and practically speaking exploded, committing suicide right there in front of the eyes of the butchers.

> I am more astonished that "scientists" are surprised that animals may actually have feelings and emotions. Perhaps the blinkers are at last beginning to come off - it's long been the human animal that is devoid of emotion.
> ~Ken, Durham

The butcher told Gagik Buniatyan that he believed that this animal had much intelligence. He remembered that when he was looking into the bull's eyes, it seemed as it the bull was talking to him, cursing him for what he was doing to him and to the other animals. The butcher added that he could never forget the incident, the eyes and the feeling of that bull.

> *Tit for tat. One who is going to commit violence unnecessarily, the king, government, should immediately take the sword and kill that person. That is government's duty. Had it been Vedic culture prevailing now, all these persons who are unnecessarily killing the cows in the slaughterhouse, they would have been killed by the king.*
> ~**Srila Prabhupada** *(Lecture, Bhagavad-gita 2.36-37, London, September 4, 1973)*

18.

Cows Are Intensely Emotional

Despite appearing unexpressive by human standards, cows are a sophisticated bunch who communicate with each other on many levels. Under natural circumstances, cows live in herds with social hierarchies and form lifelong bonds with each other. Many researchers have found that cows even have the capacity to worry about the future.

When they are separated from their families, friends, or human companions, cows grieve over the loss. Researchers report that cows become visibly distressed after even a brief separation from a loved

one. Cows are especially dedicated to their young and the bond formed between a mother and her calf remains long after the baby has grown to adulthood. Separation causes them tremendous stress and agitation. If mother and calf are separated by a fence, the mother will wait for her calf, even through harsh conditions like intense heat or cold weather, hunger and thirst.

> *I'm afraid that our feelings of superiority are taught by our elitist religions. Fortunately, animals have no such absurd impediments.*
> *~Jimsberg, USA*

Cows have even been known to break fences and walk miles to be reunited with calves that were sold at auction. One can imagine the trauma a dairy cow must feel when her calf is taken from her shortly after birth. It's well known to farmers but rarely discussed that mother cows continue to frantically call and search for their babies for days after the calves have been sold off to veal farms.

Not surprisingly, studies have found that cows recognize and respond to kind treatment from humans. Edmund Pajor of Purdue University said that cows will actually produce significantly more milk when they are spoken to gently than they do when shouted at and handled roughly. According to Purdue's findings, it doesn't take much for the cows to feel badly – they reacted poorly to even a simple slap on the rump meant to keep them moving. Cows don't forget being hurt and seem to hold grudges not only against other cows, but also against people who have hurt them or their family members.

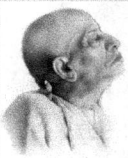

Maharaja Pariksit was actually an ideal saintly king because while touring his kingdom he happened to see that a poor cow was about to be killed by the personified Kali, whom he at once took to task as a murderer. This means that even the animals were given protection by the saintly administrators, not from any sentimental point of view, but because those who have taken their birth in the material world have the right to live.
~Srila Prabhupada (Srimad Bhagavatam 1.12.19p)

19.

Cow Feeds Baby Goats

In November 2009, a cow in Orissa province of India, attracted medida's attention for her exhibition of love and affection.

The cow in the Jagatsinghpur village of Orissa became a celebrity for feeding two baby goats. Hundreds of onlookers were visiting the village, about 80 km from state capital Bhubaneswar, to witness this rare sight. The owner, Manguli Bhoi's cow was feeding the goats for half an hour every day and licking them clean.

Mr Bhoi is the owner of both the cow and the goats. He has one shed where he keeps his livestock. One of the goats gave birth to

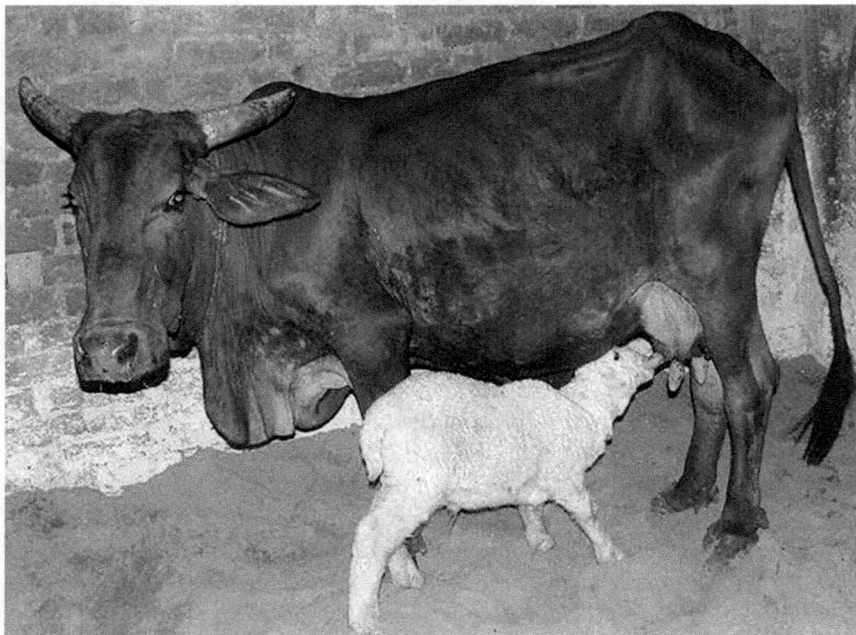

four kids three months ago. She rejected and stopped feeding two of them a month later as she was weak and not able to produce enough milk.

Cows long ago resolved that very contentious issue, care of the young. Any herd with several calves has a crèche or calf care centre. Calves gather in a selected spot under the watchful protection of two or three cows. The rest of the mammas go off happily grazing, confident that their little ones are safe. Childcare isn't a feminist plot; it's female wisdom in the bovine species.
~Trudy

The hungry babies approached the cow and she readily offered them her milk. People around were astonished to see the baby goats get nourishment from the cow.

Hundreds of people from nearby villages have been thronging to witness this unique display of love and affection by the cow.

Vedic literatures rightly put it, 'gavo visvasya matarah', cow is the mother of all living beings in this universe.

20.
Some Facts About Cows !

C ows can communicate with each other by "mooing" frequently. This helps them keep in contact, especially when it is dark. Cows also communicate through a wide variety of physical movements and facial expressions.

Cows have been known to form lifelong friendships.

Cows will look out for the old and weak members of the herd. When dairy cows return to be milked, a leader is selected to guide the way.

Their mother's milk and good exercise are crucial to the growth of a happy calf. In a natural environment, a calf nurses for up to eight months (much more than the few days or hours that factory farms allow). This is how the calf receives all the nutrients it needs and develops its immunities. The calf's strength and coordination

are built through playing with other calves.

In western terminology, cow is a term used to describe female cattle that have given birth. Females who have not yet had any babies are called heifers. Males are called bulls and the young are known as calves.

Cows have excellent senses of hearing and smell. They can hear high and low frequencies better than humans, and can detect odors from as far away as 8km.

I have my 10 cows in Sri lanka. I am planing to feed children a free glass of milk a day. I have 100 kids in my village school. I want them to learn how important it is to appreciate all the animal on earth. They are very dependable. They are very precious. Can you imagine how boring life would be if only people were around you without any animals or birds? Please email me at ilovemy10cows@yahoo.com
~Roshan Goonathilake

A cow's coat is like a snowflake – each spot on a cow is unique so no two cows are exactly alike.

Cows living in herds will cooperate to protect all their young.

The protection of cows maintains the most miraculous form of food, i.e., milk for maintaining the finer tissues of the brain for understanding higher aims of life.
~Srila Prabhupada (Srimad Bhagavatam 1.8.5)

21.

This One Is 'Paan' Fanatic!

A motley crowd of amused onlookers gathers outside a tiny kiosk selling "Paan", an Indian mouth-freshener made out of betel leaf, for their daily dose of entertainment.

Located in India's western Rajkot town, the owner of 'Shanker Paan Corner' plays host to a very special client, who has since become a minor celebrity.

A chestnut-coloured cow, fondly named "Gauri" (another name for the consort of Lord Shiva, Hindu God of destruction) is also a paan fanatic.

It's people who generally eat paan, but when people see the cow relishing the paan, they are taken aback. The shop owner says she had been coming to his shop since the last three years.

The owner of the shop, Jagadish Jawahar, who coincidentally carries a tattoo of a cow on his hand, considers his relation with Gauri to be "divine".

Jagadish, the kiosk owner used to bring a "roti" (Indian pancake) for the cow everyday. But once he forgot to bring the "roti". So he

Krishna is habituated to take care of the cows. Just like nowadays any respectable gentleman is supposed to take care of dog.
~Srila Prabhupada (Lecture, Jakarta, February 27, 1973)

thought what should he give her and then decided to offer her a paan. This became a daily occurrence and now it's nearly three years. "She normally likes the sweet variety," says Jagadish.

She visits him at least five times a day, just like any other paan aficionado, and satisfies her urge for the betel leaf spiked with various masalas. She will leave only after tasting her daily dose of mouth watering Paan, otherwise stand adamant there.

She hasn't missed her visit to the shop for a single day. She arrives exactly at the same time, and in all weather conditions.

COWS ARE SO COOL...
Where would we be with out them?
Cows are the best animal that ever lived!
my favorite animal is a cow! you would know that by seeing my room!
~Karen, Memphis USA

It is a great entertainment for a lot of onlookers who would stand still lest they disturb her from enjoying that pleasure. None of them leaves the sight until they finish watching her relish her paan with closed eyes.

That Gauri is part of a larger species revered in the country as holy mother only makes matters easier for the bovine as the owner does not demand or expect charges for his services.

It still makes me emotional. I don't know if you have ever looked into a cow's eye, but it is so soulful.
~ Hilary Swank (Oscar-award winning actress)

22.

Kids And Cows

In Ancient India

Five thousand years ago, Lord Krishna incarnated in the holy land of Mathura in India. Srila Prabhupada gives the following description of His pastimes as a cowherd boy.

"Nanda Maharaja, the foster father of Krsna, was keeping 900,000 cows. And He was rich man. He was maharaja, king. But see the behavior. His beloved son, Krsna and Balarama, he has entrusted to take care of the calves or cows: "Go in the forest." He is well dressed with ornament, and nice dress, everything. All the cowherds boys, they are very rich. They have got enough grains and enough milk. Naturally they will be rich. But not that the cows and the calves will be taken care of by some hired servant. No. They would take care himself.

That was children's sport, to go to the forest, take the calves and cows and carry some tiffin. Eat there, dance there, play there, and again come in the evening. Then they will take bath and change their dress and take their meals and immediately go to sleep. This was the boy's, children's, engagement. So how they would grow healthy because they go outside and play and work and very happily, they enjoy the company. So there is no question of becoming contaminated. Yamuna-tira-vana-cari. Yamuna-tira, on the bank of the Yamuna... Just like we go to the seaside, the beach, similarly, there is bank of Yamuna, very nice river, and there are trees. So these boys, Krsna and His friends, with their cows they will go and loiter on the bank of the Yamuna and sport and frivolities, everything, so nicely. So there was no question of education at that time. After the child is grown up, healthy, nice, then he goes to school. Otherwise first of all eat sumptuously milk, butter and yogurt, and play sufficiently in open air with friends, take care of the cows. This is labor. But it is sporting, very nice. So these things were taught by Krsna Himself, although He was the son of king.
(Lecture, Srimad-Bhagavatam 1.9.2, Los Angeles, May 16, 1973)

How egocentric of humans to think we are the only beings who can think, feel, bond with others, etc. As the "dominating" species, we have a responsibility to care for and protect the entire planet, including the other animals.
~Sioux Komoroski, Tucson, Arizona, USA

Theres 2 cows in a field, One cow looks at the other cow and says "moo." The other cow looks back and says "I was just going to say that"

23.

Cows Love This 8 Years Old Girl

And She Loves 'Em

At just 8-years old, Brittani Burke of South Windsor in Connecticut, United States, is a cow fanatic. She just loves to be around the cows and work with them every day.

Brittani owns four cows, and in between her time as a second-grader at Philip R. Smith School and helping out around her family's farm and nursery, she spends most of her free time training and caring for the animals.

Her four cows are named Maddie, Molly, Milie and Manny. "I try to spend as much time with the cows as I can," Brittani says, as she scratched Maddie's belly with a stick.

"I like how I can play with the animals and have fun with them, but sometimes I get frustrated," Brittani says. "If you don't have lots of patience you'll get very angry."

> *Humans are so embarrassingly egocentric. So many confuse an animal's inability to communicate in a human way with not having thoughts or emotions at all. Thank goodness somebody is doing something to show otherwise.*
> *~Betsy, San Marcos, TX, U.S.A.*

And a 1,400-pound angry Maddie isn't easy to control when she's annoyed, but someone's always there to help Brittani.

Brittani likes to compete with her cows in the shows in her state. She won Grand Champion Angus Female with Maddie this year. Her champion, 2-year-old Maddie, won five competitions this summer in various classes. But Brittani says, "I don't care if I win. I just want some nice cows."

She's been showing cows since she was 2 years old, and each year she takes on more and more of the exhausting work it takes to get the cows ready for a show. The animals have to be trained to stand the right way, walk at the right pace, get used to people and keep their head up, not an easy feat when instinct tells them to keep it down for grazing.

That's all before the beauty pageant part of the contest, where each cow has to be perfectly groomed, washed and combed. When it's all done Maddie is soft "like little cotton balls."

She is taking more and more responsibility for the cows. She does

> *Despite living in a city I totally want a cow!! A black and white and miniature cows!! I once lived next to a cow farm of some sorts for the summer in Texas! We would moo and they would stampede to the edge of the property close to the fences! We would feed them gourds and such. I don't know why they'd always come when we called them. It was heaven!!! I guess I should find some sort of mountain man, so that we can own cows together!! I'm not a strict veg but trying hard to become one... and the cows I own would be my pets.!! But I sooo want a cow!!*
> *Mary J. Foley, San Jose, March 19, 2006,*

all the washing right now. Every year she is taking a bigger and bigger step and learning more and more. And when she isn't working with Maddie or Molly, or Milie, or Manny, Brittani likes to dance, sing and ride horses.

Brittani plans to keep on showing her animals, including 4-year-old Molly, Maddie's mother, who was "my first cow and my favorite."

Eventually, she wants to work the family farm and keep participating in shows. But for now she'll keep learning and trying to raise the best cows she can.

"It takes years to develop a herd. We've been working on this blood line for long time," she proudly explains.

24.

Study: Cows Excel At Selecting Leaders

Recent studies on leadership in cows and other grazing herbivores suggest that intelligence, inquisitiveness, confidence, experience and good social skills help to determine which animals will become leaders within herds.

The findings suggest that, at least among these animals, individuals are not necessarily "born leaders," and that bullying, selfishness, size and strength are not recognized as suitable leadership qualities.

Bertrand Dumont, lead author of a recent *Applied Animal Behavior Science* paper on leadership in a group of grazing cows, explains, "The

fact that in groups of animals of different age, leaders are amongst the oldest animals suggests that it's not innate, but the result of previous experience." Dumont is a researcher at the national institute of agricultural research in France.

He adds, "Usually leadership and dominance are not correlated. In other words, leaders are not the strongest animals." Dumont and his team observed a group of 15 two-year-old cows at a farm in France. During the day, the cows were allowed to graze on a rectangular plot of cocksfoot-covered land that was separated from another plot by an alleyway.

I think people should stop harming cows because eating a cow would be like eating you and wearing a cows fur would be like wearing you. They are not a part of the food group/chain.
~Taylor M. Scott

This second plot was planted with patches of ryegrass, which the cows particularly like to eat.

Whenever the herd was allowed access to this new feeding site, cow #7 usually was the first to investigate. When she was with the herd and then moved toward the new food site again, the other cows appeared to acknowledge her judgment and followed behind her in distinct social groupings of three or so cows.

This shows that affinities probably exist between particular animals, and that #7 might have had past success at leading the herd to new food sites. It's adaptive to the animals to follow successful leaders, as this will improve their own food research success.

The researchers could not detect any obvious signaling by #7 before the rest of the herd followed her lead. Prior studies indicate bovines actually vote on which direction the herd should take by communicating with each other via body language.

Derek Bailey, associate professor of animal and range sciences at New Mexico State University, explains that the bovines orient their bodies toward the desired direction of movement. The bovines then go where the most animals are pointed.

Bailey, who agrees with Dumont's observation that leaders are individuals that other animals follow to a food source, has conducted similar research on cattle in Montana.

Bravo! I thought that when I was a teenager writing essays for school about my pet cows (I raised 2 calves as a project) I was alone in ascribing thoughts and feelings to them but now about 60 years later I feel vindicated! Thanks.
Marie Morgan, Tucson, Arizona, USA

"One cow in particular — her identification number was 2232 — was always in front of the herd, always one of the first three animals," Bailey says. "We used this cow to help us move less cooperative animals out of pastures."

He thinks cows that convey a sense of purpose and confidence often become leaders. Cows, unlike humans, are not subject to false bravado, so usually cattle confidence is founded on intelligence. Purposeful movement may result from knowledge of a good location to forage and as a result, may be a signal to other animals.

In future, Dumont and his colleagues hope to determine what specific movements, or other tactics, bovine leaders might use before instigating group movement.

By Jennifer Viegas, Animal Planet News

Of all kinds of animal killing, the killing of cows is most vicious because the cow gives us all kinds of pleasure by supplying milk. Cow slaughter is an act of the grossest type of ignorance. In the Vedic literature (Rg Veda 9.46.4) the words gobhih prinita-matsaram indicate that one who, being fully satisfied by milk, is desirous of killing the cow is in the grossest ignorance.
~Srila Prabhupada (Bhagavad-gita 14.16)

25.

Bulls - An Observation
By Trudy Frisk

It was a sight to make a cowherd boy rejoice. Two fearsome bulls faced each other. Dust swirled in clouds as they pawed the ground. Menacing bellows resounded throughout the valley. A circle of admiring cows watched in eager anticipation. Nature at work on the farm.

Hah! After half an hour of snorting and stamping the 'rival' bulls buddied up and, shoulder to shoulder, strolled down to the water-hole for a drink leaving the chagrined and disappointed cows glaring after them.

During my twelve year's close observation of bulls on the farm such sad scenes have been commonplace. Often cows are batting their eyelashes, asking the bull's astrological sign to get his attention. The result? Indifference. And, it's taking a toll on the cows.

Remember the stern, dedicated bulls of bygone days? Bulls with a good work ethic and strong sense of duty. Given a chore to perform they promptly and skillfully did it. They roamed the range, guarding the herd from coyotes, bears or opportunist poachers. May be neglect, and commercialization of farms is responsible for laziness of the bulls!

(Trudy Frisk is a freelance writer living in Kamloops, B.C., Canada)

26.

An Old Cow Tugs At Millions of Heartstrings

Story of A 40 Years Old South Korean Cow And Her Farmer

To a South Korean farmer, this cow was sacred

A South Korean film made instant stars of two elderly farmers and their aged cow. South Korean farmer Choi Won-kyun and wife Lee Sam-sun became overnight celebrities in South Korea after their appearance in a documentary film that broke box-office records there. Many theatres in US and Europe are also screening this film.

They're the unlikely stars of "Old Partner," a documentary film that chronicles two years in the lives of the hard-working couple as

they live with their aging cow that has served them faithfully for 40 years. It's title in Korean is 'wo-nang-so-ri', 'The Sound of the Cow's Bell.'

The movie shattered box-office records in Korea for an independent film, becoming an instant low-budget classic, a fable about love, loyalty and rural Korean values — and also a touching, sometimes funny, tale of a wife's jealousy over the bond between husband and the cow.

The movie portrays what might be one of the last stories of heartbreaking sacrifice and the touching interaction between a cow and its owner in the down slopes of life

The story has left people of all ages teary-eyed, including First Lady Kim Yoon-ok, who with President Lee Myung-bak recently showed up unexpectedly at a Seoul theater to watch the film.

The film seems out of place in a world of fast-paced images and breathtaking special effects. Instead, it seems more like a collection of still shots strung together than like a moving picture, as it portrays the life of an old man as he spends his final days with his cow as it dies of old age.

Man meets cow. Man loses cow. Man finds cow again - while not exactly adhering to that old Hollywood narrative technique, it is definitely a peculiar but heartwarming story.

Dull as it may sound, this low-budget movie has topped the country's box office charts, a first for an independent film here. Many are left wondering as to how such a slow-paced story can become the most-watched independent film in Korea, drawing more than 2 million viewers just six weeks after its premiere. According to Variety, only $142,000 was spent to make and market the film, a mere pittance by Hollywood standards.

"Now the cow's status has changed. They're no longer family members but seen as pieces of meat."
~Lee Chung-ryul, Film Director

A Romantic Triangle

The farmer says, "This cow is better than a human. When it dies, I'll be its chief mourner — and I'll follow. I'm alive because of this cow."

If I die, you live... If you die, I live...

Thank you, Dear my

old 우심리
partner

Later, the farmer Choi sits forlornly with his head in his arms as his wife gripes that he loves the cow more than he loves her. He doesn't react, but when the animal lows, his head jerks up.

"It was a romantic triangle," says director Lee. "The old woman was jealous because her husband gave the cow more attention."

The cow is the 80-year-old man's best friend, his only farming machine, and his only means of transportation. He rides to his fields every day in a small cart attached to his bovine friend.

Even as the animal, at the age of 40, is in its final days (most cows live to 15), it toils until it can no longer walk or stand. Meanwhile the farmer Choi, hobbles around in search of grass to feed his cow. He also refuses to use pesticides on his crops, fearing he might poison his friend.

That simple, touching plot is working with audiences worldwide.

"It feels like I've just heard a beautiful poem," said 47-year-old

Shin Yong-shik, after walking out of the cinema with his son and wife. "As the world around us becomes more harsh and urbanized this film reminds people of parts of life that are slowly disappearing."

Thus a low budget tale of bovine-human love captivates South Korea and rest of the world.

I find it enormously puzzling that extreme suffering only gets widely questioned if it is the suffering of members of the human species. It is extraordinary how many people just accept the appalling treatment of such a vast number of animals.

Dr David Pearson, Lancaster, UK

Fame That Disrupts Their Simple Life

But since the movie's January premiere, a near-daily invasion of curious visitors has threatened the tranquil life of the village couple, who just want to be left alone. Everyone wants a piece of them, pestering for countless photos: Stand here. Pose there. Bale more hay. Smile! Now take us to the old cow's grave site for just a few more snapshots. The boldest intruders barge into the house uninvited.

And the stampede to see South Korea's most reluctant celebrities starts early, often before they're out of bed.

On many weekends, hundreds of tourists appear at the tumbledown homestead to meet 82-year-old farmer Choi Won-kyun and his loving but nagging wife, Lee Sam-sun.

Choi Won-kyun, the eldest of the couple's nine children says, "I'm gratified that people are interested in my parents. If only they would have a sip of coffee and leave, but they stay. What can my parents do? Hospitality is part of rural life. We don't have any choice but to welcome them."

you are ungrateful. You are drinking milk, you are taking so much butter, milk product, and as gratitude you are killing cows? You should be ashamed. Even if you have no human feelings. You suck the breast of your mother and kill? Is that humanity?
~Srila Prabhupada (Bhagavad-gita 3.11-19, Los Angeles, December 27, 1968)

The director recently made a nationwide appeal to South Koreans to respect the couple's privacy. But the hordes keep coming.

If it weren't for people, cattle would be happy in the wild, but now the fact that cattle are profitable for people to farm is the only thing standing between bovine and oblivion. A good farmer loves his cattle and does not rest himself unless they are taken care of. Look at factory farming and 25000 head feedlots for a real source of oblivious cruelty. ~Christine Roussel

The local tourism board is planning an "Old Partner" museum and has erected signs leading to the farm.

It has collected the elder Choi's clothes and cane used in the movie. The board even claimed the tarnished cowbell, with plans to sell replicas to tourists.

Unexpected Success At The Box Office

The project brought first-time director Lee Chung-ryul overnight success. He says. "This movie has become more successful than I ever imagined. It has taken on a life of its own."

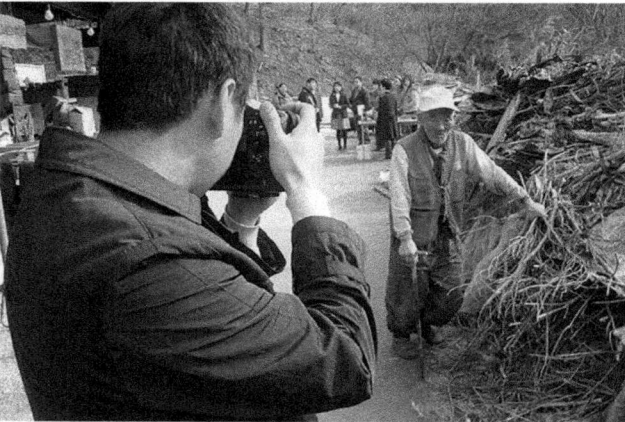

Lee wanted to make a documentary about the beauty of simple things. To tell the story, he chose a farmer who preferred his devoted old cow over any modern tractor.

He was inspired by his own rural childhood and the novelist Pearl S. Buck, who nearly a century ago wrote of a farmer and cow she saw on a trip to Korea. "Now the cow's status has changed. They're no longer family members but seen as pieces of meat", laments Lee.

Cow And Humanity - A Natural Relationship

For five years, he searched for the right subject for his film. In 2002, he was introduced to the Farmer Choi, who recently had been informed that his female ox's days were numbered. She had already lived far longer than most.

The pair's similarities astounded him: Nearly deaf with a malformed leg, the limping farmer was often forced to crawl across

his rice fields. The staggering brown cow, which is never given a name, was no better off. Choi often groomed the skinny animal's diseased hide and fed her special gruel to keep her strength up.

For Lee, the pair seemed to have a secret pact: Keep working together or we'll both die.

In 2005, he began shooting what he saw as an intimate chronicle of the cow's final year. Problems arose from day one.

Choi resisted any intrusion he felt would interrupt his chores.

With kind treatment, cows can be very loyal companions. In her book Peaceful Kingdom: Random Acts of Kindness by Animals, Stephanie Laland writes that when the Rev. O. F. Robertson began to go blind, his cow Mary became his "seeing-eye cow." Mary would walk along with him, nudging him away from obstacles. She accompanied Robertson everywhere he went for the rest of his life.

Every time Lee approached with his camera, Choi and his wife stopped talking, or stared as though posing for a snapshot.

So the director affixed microphones to the couple's clothes and filmed from a distance with a zoom lens.

> *Reading about cows feels like hearing some news about old friends. I knew few individual cows. I haven't been out to volunteer in a long time. I miss them. Cows are kind, patient, beautiful individuals.*
> *~Mark Middleton*

What his camera captured was a poignant real-life drama, as the woman constantly berated her husband for not exchanging his old partner for a tractor.

In her gravelly voice, she nags him to use chemicals that would improve crop yields and about the energy he wastes doting on the cow — but especially about her tiring labors caring for both animal and husband.

"We work so hard," she tells the cow one day. "We both met the wrong man."

Passing Away of The Cow - The Final Plot

As the animal grows weaker, the couple and cow seem to know the end is near. In one sequence, Lee shows a tear in the eye of the farmer, then his wife, then the cow.

In one of their last days together, the animal struggles during a trip to collect firewood, prompting the farmer to stop the cart. He unloads some of the wood, straps it to his back and walks alongside his old partner in a gesture that signals he considers the two equals.

But Lee, the director, couldn't be there for every poignant moment. He wasn't there when the cow finally fell over, unable to rise.

Alerted by the farmer's eldest son, he made the three-hour journey from Seoul to find Choi weeping as he implored the cow to get up, asking a veterinarian, "What can I do to prolong its life?"

When the animal finally dies, even the wife is moved. "May you go to heaven," she says. "But why are you leaving before us?"

Finally, Lee had his ending. He went into postproduction, creating movie posters that showed the farmer's weathered hands holding his keepsake cowbell. In Korean, the film is called "The Sound of the Cow's Bell."

Success was immediate. The movie won an award at the prestigious Busan International Film Festival and played at the Sundance Film Festival.

South Korea's previous box-office record for an independent documentary was 120,000 tickets but this film surpassed 3 million. Even President Lee Myung-bak wanted to meet the director.

"One morning I woke up famous," Lee recalls.

Cow Has A Natural Appeal To Human Soul

The film's success has surprised many because the box office is dominated by Hollywood blockbusters and local movies that are increasingly costly to produce.

One might say that the themes were a bit too serious to attract the public in large numbers. As a low-budgeted movie (produced at around $142,000) there were no big names nor any special effects.

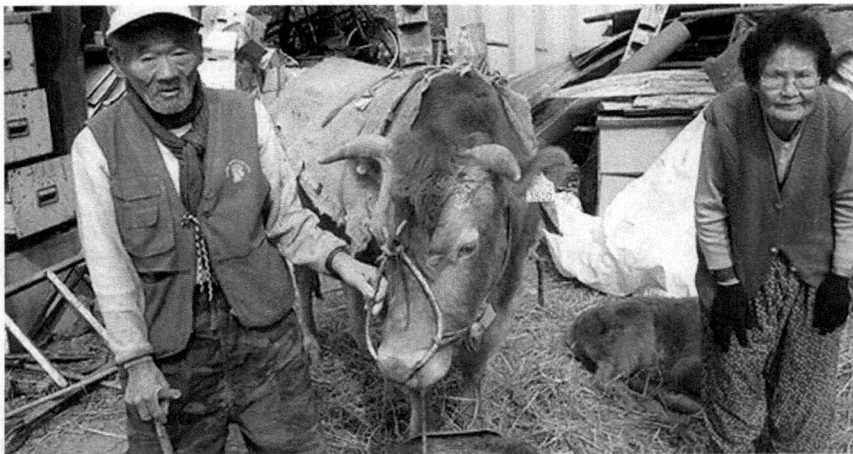

One might wonder how it could draw almost 2 million people in its six weeks of showing when the competing Hollywood movie at local theatres that time was starring Brad Pitt and was an Oscar-nominee. The answer is - cow and land based simple life has a direct appeal to human soul. The heroes of this movie - the farmer and his wife, know only two things in their life, cow and farming. In fact throughout their lives they have known only these two things. This is the natural plan of living and though we have distanced ourselves from this natural plan due to urbanization and industrialization, the craving, the yearning to return to our original nature remains. That is the reasons, millions could relate to the film's plot even though it has no action, no drama, no special effects. But it has one thing for sure - direct appeal to your soul, to your essential nature.

I worked on a dairy farm and at this one period, when the cows were being kept in the stanchions in a long row, there was this first cow that would hold her head in the water trough to let the water run over for the longest time, till the alley was full of water all of the time. Then one day we found that the drinking cup for the cow at the end of the row did not work. As soon as we noticed this and fixed it, the first cow no longer held her face down to cause it to over flow... I was amazed.
Maureen J Valenti, San Angelo, Texas, USA

27.

Cow's Cradle

By Sarah Rath

A friend tells me that like most young farm wives she went to the barn for milking, even with a small baby to tend.

Baby was a fussy one and would bring the sky down if left unattended for a moment.

But she had her own unique way of handling the situation.

They were fortunate to have an old fashioned cradle that she took down to the barn.

The baby was placed in the cradle, with one end of a rope tied to the cradle and the other end of the rope tied to a cow's tail.

And as the cow switched her tail, the cradle was rocked. And the cow was milked.

(Rath, Sarah. *About Cows. Minocqua, WI:*NorthWood Press, Inc., 1987)

28.

Sweet Music for Milking

As per psychologists at the University of Leicester, UK, who played music of different tempos to herds of Friesian cows, dairy cows produce more milk when listening to relaxing music. They believe farmers could get an extra pint from their charges by playing classical music or slow numbers in the cowshed.

Beethoven's Pastoral Symphony and Simon & Garfunkel's Bridge Over Troubled Water were a big hit in the milking shed. But when rowdy numbers, like Mud's Tigerfeet and Size of a Cow by Wonderstuff, were played, there was no increase in milk yield.

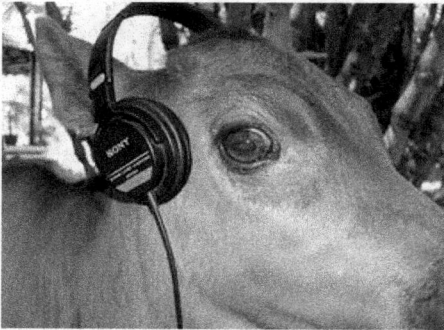

Dr Adrian North, who carried out the study with colleague Liam MacKenzie says, "Calming music can improve milk yield, because it reduces stress."

I think that in 100 years, people will look back in wonder that we could not recognize animal's feelings and view it as we now view historical figures who thought that Native Americans had no souls, or that slavery was God's plan. This blindness is the same factor that prevents us from recognizing the humanity of those with whom we go to war. In order to continue to believe in a moral world (that conveniently works to our advantage), we have to devalue those whom we exploit or kill for resources.
~Pat Hakes, Safety Harbor, Florida, US

Some farmers already play music to chickens, as there is anecdotal evidence that it reduces stress.

Dr North took the lead when he saw many farmers believe that music can boost milk production.

Stress Relief

The study was carried out at LCAH Dairies in Lincolnshire and Bishop Burton Agricultural College in Humberside.

One-thousand-strong herds of Friesian cows were exposed to fast, slow and no music for 12 hours a day, from 5am to 5pm, over the course of nine weeks.

The researchers found that each cow's milk yield rose by 3% (0.73 litres) a day when slow music, rather than fast music, was played.

Cows are gorgeous !
I love all animals but cows are the best. They are so neat and gentle and their huge eyes. I gave up eating meat after my parents sent my cow to the works this year. I worked on a dairy farm so cruel but I didn't let any calves go on the bobby truck. I got homes for them all.
~Edward Hill, Norway

The work adds to evidence that calming music reduces stress in animals, as well as people. Most theories of music preferences are based on humans.

It was found that slow music improved milk yields perhaps because it relaxes the cows in much the same way as it relaxes humans.

The researchers are now seeking further funding to see whether music can help other animals.

"Turning cows into 'blue suede shoes' and slabs of beef ignores the fact that cows want to live and enjoy their lives, just as humans do,"
~Tracy Reiman (Executive Vice President, PETA)

Cows are sedentary creatures. They like to eat grass, stand still and occasionally moo. And they don't like to rock. However, they do seem to enjoy calming pop ballads. However, faster songs seemed to trouble the animals, slightly reducing their milk yield.

A 10 Year Old Boy Solved The Weak Milk Production Problem

Daniel McElmurray from Hephzibah, Georgia, recently won first place in a regional science fair for a project on how music improved milk production in cows.

After hearing his dad, Earl complained about weak milk production from their 300 cows, the 10-year-old student at Goshen Elementary in Augusta helped solve the problem with a prize-winning science fair project.

He tested the effects of classical, country and rock music on the cows.

Daniel says he and his dad like to listen to music while they milk the cows, without giving the cows much say in the selection.

Turns out rock is their least favorite. After listening to Lynyrd Skynyrd, Shania Twain and a selection of classical music, the cows

kamam vavarsa parjanyah
sarva-kama-dugha mahi
sisicuh sma vrajan gavah
payasodhasvatir muda
During the reign of Maharaja Yudhisthira, the clouds showered all the water that people needed, and the earth produced all the necessities of man in profusion. Due to its fatty milk bag and cheerful attitude, the cow used to moisten the grazing ground with milk. (Srimad Bhagavatam 1.10.4)

proved they prefer classical to country and rock by producing 1,000 pounds more milk.

He received a special award from the American Society of Mammalogists, an organization that supports the study of mammals.

I don't know why or how,
God decided to make the cow
with its belly oh so white
and a brain thats not so bright
Eating grass
and sleep sound
all day long on the ground

by Nathan

29.

Happy Cows, Happy Society

"How now brown cow?"

This is a phrase used sometimes in UK as a greeting. This is equivalent to asking - how are you? That would mean, if cow is fine, so you are and if cow is not, you too are not.

This is about a modern country but in many traditional cultures also, well-being of cattle is taken to be the well-being of human beings. For example, in Mongolian culture, on meeting an acquaintance, or even a stranger, the Mongol salutes him with, 'How are your cattle?' This is always one of the first questions, and they make no enquiry after your health until they have learned that your cows, sheep, camels, and horses are fat and well to do.

Also in Vedic tradition, while describing the condition of a society, very often just the condition of cows and bulls is mentioned. Cows

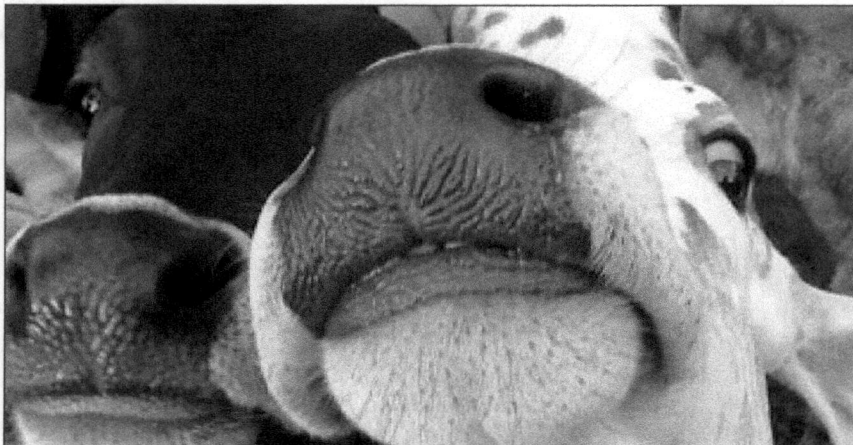

and bulls are considered to be a barometer which gauges the happiness and well-being of a society.

Srimad Bhagavatam, a Vedic text, describes the rule of Pandava dynasty in India 5000 years ago:

"During the reign of Maharaja Yudhisthira, the clouds showered all the water that people needed, and the earth produced all the necessities of man in profusion. Due to its fatty milk bag and cheerful attitude, the cow used to moisten the grazing ground with milk."(SB 1.10.4)

> *Ok I may just really sound like a freak. ...well I love cows. They are so cute and useful. Without cows there would be no milky ice creams, no milky cheese, no milkshakes, no milky chocolate, no white chocolate, no cheese, no yogurts!*
> *How would this world cope?*
> *-Sandra Hall, Jacksonville*

There is no description of populace but cows are described as 'cheerful'. From this the people's well-being and their peaceful condition is to be inferred. Happy cows give away their milk in plenty and cheerful bulls do all kinds of work. Sufficient supply of cow products ensure healthy minds, healthy brains and healthy bodies. Not only human beings but all living creatures can thus live peacefully and execute the mission of life. In such a society, there is perfect harmony between man, animals, nature and God. People live a life of freedom from physical ailments and mental agonies.

> *The bull is the emblem of the moral principle, and the cow is the representative of the earth. When the bull and the cow are in a joyful mood, it is to be understood that the people of the world are also in a joyful mood. The reason is that the bull helps production of grains in the agricultural field, and the cow delivers milk, the miracle of aggregate food values. The human society, therefore, maintains these two important animals very carefully so that they can wander everywhere in cheerfulness. But at the present moment in this age of Kali both the bull and the cow are now being slaughtered and eaten up as foodstuff by a class of men who do not know the brahminical culture.*
> *~Srila Prabhupada (Srimad Bhagavatam 1.16.18)*

We can cite another instance from Srimad Bhagavatam which relates to the meeting of two friends, Nanda and Vasudeva. Nanda was the leader of a cowherd community and Vasudeva was a dethroned king. As soon as they met, Vasudeva enquired from Nanda, "Please tell me about the welfare of Vrndavana. You have many animals -- are they happy? Are they getting sufficient grass and water? Please also let me know whether the place where you are now living is undisturbed and peaceful."

Srila Prabhupada comments on this episode, "It is also significant that Vasudeva inquired about the welfare of Nanda Maharaja's animals. The animals, and especially the cows, were protected exactly in the manner of one's children. Vasudeva was a ksatriya, and Nanda Maharaja was a vaisya. It is the duty of the ksatriyas to give protection to the citizens, and it is the duty of the vaisyas to give protection to the cows. The cows are as important as the citizens. Just as the human citizens should be given all kinds of protection, so the cows also should be given full protection." *(Krishna Book 5: The Meeting of Nanda and Vasudeva)*

> *yas tvam krsne gate duram*
> *saha-gandiva-dhanvana*
> *socyo 'sy asocyan rahasi*
> *praharan vadham arhasi*
>
> *You rogue, do you dare beat an innocent cow because Lord Krsna and Arjuna, the carrier of the Gandiva bow, are out of sight? Since you are beating the innocent in a secluded place, you are considered a culprit and therefore deserve to be killed.*
>
> *In a civilization where God is conspicuously banished, and there is no devotee warrior like Arjuna, the associates of the age of Kali take advantage of this lawless kingdom and arrange to kill innocent animals like the cow in secluded slaughterhouses. Such murderers of animals stand to be condemned to death by the order of a pious king like Maharaja Pariksit. For a pious king, the culprit who kills an animal in a secluded place is punishable by the death penalty, exactly like a murderer who kills an innocent child in a secluded place. (Srimad Bhagavatam 1.17.6)*

30.

Holy Cow! De-stressing Is So Simple

Maulana Wahiduddin Khan

I was a student of a village madrassa in Uttar Pradesh in the 1930s. We studied a poem by the renowned poet Ismail Meerathi in the Urdu reader.

It was titled 'Hamari Gaay' - Our Cow. One of the verses went like this:

"Kal jo ghas chari thi ban mein,
Doodh bani woh gaay ke than mein."

It means that the cow is a special kind of animal. It takes (eats) grass and in return gives us milk. In other words, the cow is divine; it is able to convert non-milk into milk.

This poem became a part of my memory. It taught me a great lesson. God, the Creator, has made the cow a model for human

The two learned scholars began a long discussion on the Koran and Hindu sastras. The Lord raised the question of cow-killing, and the Kazi properly answered Him by referring to the Koran. In turn the Kazi also questioned the Lord about cow sacrifice in the Vedas, and the Lord replied that such sacrifice as mentioned in the Vedas is not actually cow-killing. In that sacrifice an old bull or cow was sacrificed for the sake of receiving a fresh younger life by the power of Vedic mantras. But in the Kali-yuga such cow sacrifices are forbidden because there are no qualified brahmanas capable of conducting such a sacrifice.
~Srila Prabhupada (Srimad Bhagavatam, Introduction)

behaviour in that it gives us a lesson in high morality. We must develop this quality of conversion in our personality, and this should enable us to transform negative thought into positive thought.

It is said that man is a social animal. But what is society? Society is full of differences. Every day we experience provocative situations; every day we face the disagreeable behaviour of others and every day we suffer anger and tension because of conflicts arising out of differences.

I thought i was the only one! But I am so glad that there are others out there. Everyone laughs at me when I say I want a cow and that they are my favorite animal ever! How can you not love them! They are so innocent and they have those adorable long lashes! Cows Rule!
Paul Thurrott, Denver

Then what should we do? The cow could show us the answer. God has created a model in the form of the cow. We have to adopt cow culture, we have to develop in our personality what may be called the capacity for transformation; we have to turn negative experiences into positive thinking.

The fact is that everyone enjoys freedom. But everyone also has the choice to misuse freedom. It is this misuse of freedom that creates problems. Hence we need to learn the art of problem management.

gam ca dharma-dugham dinam
bhrsam sudra-padahatam
vivatsam asru-vadanam
ksamam yavasam icchatim
Although the cow is beneficial because one can draw religious principles from her, she was now rendered poor and calfless. Her legs were being beaten by a sudra. There were tears in her eyes, and she was distressed and weak. She was hankering after some grass in the field.
(Srimad Bhagavatam 1.17.3)

31.

The Path of Prosperity

Little Girl Has Better Idea Than Big Leaders

Keely is a small, 9 year old girl from the city of Mankato in Minnesota, USA. Her birthday wish is to help starving villages. With eyes closed, Keely Schuck's words could be those of a humanitarian, a sage, a saint. But open, they are simply the words of a blushing third-grader with a single birthday wish:

"I've always wanted to do something meaningful in the world."

As Keely turns 9, her wish is coming true. To celebrate her birthday day, Keely decided to forgo gifts, presents and packages. And instead, she asked friends and family to help her purchase dairy cows for starving villages worldwide.

Because cow, if not killed and eaten up, is a mobile food factory! A single cow produces many calves, in addition to manure for fertilizer and several gallons a milk each day for sustenance.

MMMMMOOOOOO!
I think that cows are so cute. They are so calm and they lick up their food and then bite it which makes it so easy to feed them. They are so cool and I love cows. I want to live in Switzerland because the Swiss love cows. Cows Rule!
~ Anna Relton, Norway

As she explains her birthday request from a sitting chair in her family's living room, her voice hardly carries beyond the coffee table. But even in tones faint and plain, her message will be heard across oceans.

Just a few weeks ago, Keely began telling friends and family about her idea of raising $500 for a hunger-relief organization where donors actually purchase food to be delivered to poverty-stricken villages around the world. The organization's goal is to provide sustainable solutions to world hunger.

> **Cows rock!**
> *Cows have been my favorite for ever. I collect tons of cow stuff and my friends always give me cow things. I think cows are the coolest animals, and are so cute.*
> ~Susan Hernandez, Glasgow

To help meet her original goal, Keely wrote and produced a short movie about her birthday wish (featuring her two younger sisters in supporting roles) and posted it on YouTube. Within days, the video had garnered nearly 600 views, and she quickly met her $500 goal.

Now, she's hoping to raise $1,500 — enough for three cows.

"I didn't know what I wanted for my birthday," she said. "I don't need anything. I don't want anything. ... I liked the idea of helping someone who needs help."

Kristi Schuck, Keely's mom, says she wasn't surprised by her daughter's decision. When she was only 3 years old, she remembers Keely asking Santa Claus to bring her "love" for Christmas. And another time, following a school field trip, Kristi remembers Keely remarking that she "wanted a purpose in life."

Friends, family and even strangers have responded to Keely's decision to make a difference. Keely smiles with satisfaction, "I'll remember this birthday as the year I helped change some people's lives."

Yes, donating dairy cows would be the best way to change lives. Cow is the pathway to prosperity and best form of economic development. In her life time, a cow gives thousands of gallons of milk, many calves and urine and dung which are highly useful for a village economy.

Basically living cows are better than dead ones. We are slaughtering cows to get beef. But cows give so much daily. It is just our obstinacy and ignorance that makes us kill and eat her.

In 1971 Stewart Odend'hal of the University of Missouri conducted a detailed study of cows in Bengal and found that far from depriving humans of food, they ate only inedible remains of harvested crops (rice hulls, tops of sugarcane, etc.) and grass. "Basically", he said, "the cattle convert items of little direct human value into products of immediate utility." This should put to rest the myth that people are starving in India because they will not kill their cows.

If allowed to live, cows produce High quality, protein rich foods in amounts that stagger the imagination. It is abundantly clear that cows (living ones) are one of mankind's most valuable food resources.

Little girl Kelly knows it but do our world leaders know it also?

Please Don't Shout!
Being kind to farm animals isn't just a moral duty - according to the CIWF Trust delegates; there is something in it for us, too. Cows, for example, produce significantly more milk if their handlers talk to them gently rather than shouting and pushing them around.
"The handlers don't have to be really mean and hit the cows," said Edmund Pajor of Purdue University, US. "It's just a slap on the rump in the way that many farmers would. But the cows don't like it and it makes a real difference. It helps send a message about treating animals in a proper way. A number of dairy farms now have signs up saying 'please don't shout at the cows'."

32.

Cows - Fussy About Cleanliness

By Sarah Rath

The summers could be hot in Wisconsin's Jackson County, where my family spent two weeks each summer vacationing on my grandmother's farm.

I was accustomed to swimming everyday, and found myself desperately looking for a place to cool off when I remembered the huge wooden water tank in the barnyard. I hopped into that tank and had a good cooling off, and thought nothing more about it – until my uncle started asking questions.

He wanted to know why his thirsty cows were standing around the water tank just looking, not drinking.

My uncle had to drain the tank and clean it in order to get them to drink, and that was the end of my barnyard pool.

(Rath, Sarah. *About Cows. Minocqua, WI:* NorthWood Press, Inc., 1987)

When Krishna and Balarama, with the strength of Their legs, crawled in the muddy places created in Vraja by cow dung and cow urine, Their crawling resembled the crawling of serpents, and the sound of Their ankle bells was very charming. Very much pleased by the sound of other people's ankle bells, They used to follow these people as if going to Their mothers, but when They saw that these were other people, They became afraid and returned to Their real mothers, Yasoda and Rohini.

Dressed with muddy earth mixed with cow dung and cow urine, the babies looked very beautiful, and when They went to Their mothers, both Yasoda and Rohini picked Them up with great affection, embraced Them and allowed Them to suck the milk flowing from their breasts.(Bhagavatam 10.8.22-23)

33.
Cows Moo With A Regional Accent

Recently language specialists have suggested that cows have regional accents like humans. They decided to examine the issue after dairy farmers noticed their cows had slightly different moos, depending on which herd they came from.

Cows have one word in their vocabulary and it's a single syllable at that. John Wells, Professor of Phonetics at the University of London is heading the research efforts. The farmers in Somerset who noticed the phenomenon say that it may have been the result of the close bond between them and their animals.

Farmer Lloyd Green, from Glastonbury, says: "I spend a lot of time with my cows and they definitely moo with a Somerset drawl.

Researchers spoke to the other farmers in the West Country group and they noticed a similar development in their own herds.

It all depends on the cow and farmer relationship. The closer a farmer's bond is with his cows, the easier it is for them to pick up his accent.

Peer Pressure

Prof Wells also feels that the accents could result from their contemporaries, "In small populations such as herds you would encounter identifiable dialectical variations which are most affected by the immediate peer group."

Dr Jeanine Treffers-Daller, reader in linguistics at the University of the West of England in Bristol, agreed that the accent could be influenced by relatives.

She says "When we are learning to speak, we adopt a local variety of language spoken by our parents, so the same could be said about the variation in cow moo."

Cows are great!
I love cows, they are nice to work with, they are just like humans, just not as cruel. I was once told that cows are four hoof drive, all terrain forage harvesting machines. Nothing is more enjoyable or relaxing then watching cows on a pasture.
~Rob Adams, Cape Town

The herds in the West Country are mooing in their distinct Somerset twang. Some listeners describe this sound as "moo-arr" rather than moo. Likewise in US, the cows may be having a yankeeish sounding moo.

In this British study, Brummie accents have been noticed in the Midlands, while Geordie tones abound in Tyne and Wear and there are overtones of Estuary English around the South East.

Cows are not only picking up their owners' accents and but are even passing them on to their calves. The regional twangs were first noticed by members of the West Country Farmhouse Cheesemakers group.

This Cheesemakers group is a very peculiar group. Their cheese is world famous for its unique flavour. These group members have a funny practice of spending hours with their herds, wearing cow coats and playing them classical music. The practice is supposed to contribute towards the local cheddar's distinctive flavour.

Academic Approval

The claims have received widespread academic approval.

'In small populations such as herds you would encounter dialectical variations which are most affected by the immediate peer group.'

The National Farmers' Union, UK, also backed the claims.

Livestock expert Tom Hind says: 'Cows will be used to hearing farmers shouting to bring them in with particular accents, depending on which part of the country they live in.

> *I love this. We have a lot of cattle farmers around this area of Mississippi. There are so many cute calves around. I pull over the car to look at them. They are so curious about the World around them. Cute!*
> *~Michael Allen, Mississippi*

'You could transport cows from one area of the country with a strong accent, such as Wales, to another and there could be a problem initially with them not responding to the new accent.'

Dr Margaret Rebbeck, a lecturer in material science at the University of Bradford, who made hundreds of recordings for the survey, says: 'They learn from each other and from their parents - certain phrases get passed on.'

Roses are Red

Roses are red,

Violets are blue,

if I'm a simple cow,

whats that to you?

34.

Canny Cows

By Trudy Frisk

Cows are smart. It's been said on television so it must be true. After years of being jeered at because they refused to fetch, heel, roll over or perform other humiliating tricks to please humans, cows have been recognized as having their own skills. Researchers, earlier thinking that cows make poor dogs or chimpanzees, devised tests that make sense to a cow. The results came as a surprise to many. Cows can tell the difference between a man and a woman. Even if the people change places. Even if the woman stands on a box to appear taller. There's more. After just a few lessons, cows learned to bunt a large red button with their heads to obtain grain. Cows have been moved way up the IQ ladder.

No more will the adjective 'bovine' denote something large, lethargic, placid and dim.

Where do cattle learn engineering? If there's an M.I.T., is there a B.I.T. (Bovine Institute of Technology)? Recently I noticed how easily cows find mountainous paths to reach heights for summer grazing. As any hiker who's followed a cow trail knows, cattle are unsurpassed at constructing maximum gain with minimum grade. Not for them the anguish of the steep mountains. The Sea to Sky highway leaves cows unimpressed. Cows are calm creatures. No straight up, curling round the precipice paths for them, but, cows get there. No puffing, no huffing, just steady meandering upward

According the Humane Society of the United States, if an individual cow in a herd is shocked by an electric fence, the rest will become alarmed and learn to avoid it. Only a small fraction will ever be shocked.
Some cows never forget those who have hurt them either.

avoiding obstacles while munching the occasional clump of grass.

When they're away from human scrutiny, do cows practise sneaking? I bet researchers assume cows are clumsy. Hah! One winter day a friend and I were lunching during a hike on ranch land. Not a single cow was in sight. Our attention was drawn to crashing and crackling along the dry streambed to our left. Eventually two very noisy cows appeared. When we turned back we met the inscrutable gaze of forty pairs of bovine eyes. While the scout cows in the coulee distracted us, forty of their sisters snuck silently to within ten feet of us. That's one hundred and sixty tippy-toes! They planned the diversion before they snuck. Scientists should be asking how. *(Trudy Frisk is a freelance writer living in Kamloops, B.C., Canada)*

Saunaka and the rsis were astonished to hear that the pious Maharaja Pariksit simply punished the culprit and did not kill him. This suggests that a pious king like Maharaja Pariksit should have at once killed an offender who wanted to cheat the public by dressing like a king and at the same time daring to insult the purest of the animals, a cow. The rsis in those days, however, could not even imagine that in the advanced days of the age of Kali the lowest of the sudras will be elected as administrators and will open organized slaughterhouses for killing cows.
~Srila Prabhupada (Srimad Bhagavatam 1.16.5)

35.

The 'Gentle' Bessie

By sarah Rath

It was a clear, fall evening and Father and Brother were ready to milk the cows. I asked my father if he would teach me to milk, for it was the common belief that all farm women knew how to milk. I didn't. 'Come along,' my father said.

I tagged along but when Bessie, the cow saw someone in a skirt, she rolled her eyes. Even though being the most gentle of the herd, she was suspicious of me.

Father gave me a three legged stool and a milk pail. He demonstrated how you squeeze the teat and then release in sort of rhythm. I sat down, and after a couple of squeezes, Bessie decided she'd have to do something about this. She raised up her left hind leg and stepped squarely into the pail. I jumped up, the stool fell over, and I ran. Bessie thought, 'I got rid of her.' I'll bet she smiled to herself, our Gentle Bessie.

And I remained the farmer's daughter that never learned to milk cows.

(Rath, Sarah. *About Cows. Minocqua, WI:* NorthWood Press, Inc., 1987)

The highest lifetime production of milk for a single cow is 465,224 lbs by the cow named No. 289.
The greatest amount of milk produce in one year was 59,298 lbs by a cow named Robthom Suzet Paddy.
The greatest amount of milk produced during a single day was 241 lbs by a cow named Urbe Blanca.

36.

14 Cows For America

They sing to them.
They give them names.
They shelter the young ones in their homes.
Without the herd, the tribe will die.
To The Maasai, the cow is life.

Kimeli Naiyomah, originally from Kenya, is a Stanford medical student, currently living in California. He was at the U.N. the day the twin towers fell on September 11. When he returned to Kenya, he told his Maasai tribe the story, and he asked the elders to allow him to give his only cow, named Enkarus, to the Americans. Cows are sacred to the Maasai, and this animal was meant to convey not only condolence, but also to bring healing. This was an extraordinary request, as the Maasai do not give cows to non-Maasai. In the end, the elders agreed—and then went a step further. The

tribe augmented Kimeli Naiyomah's gift with another 13 cows. The best of what they had to give.

The Maasai are an indigenous African ethnic group of semi-nomadic people located in Kenya and northern Tanzania. They are among the most well known of African ethnic groups.

Although the Tanzanian and Kenyan governments have instituted programs to encourage the Maasai to abandon their traditional semi-nomadic lifestyle, the people have continued their age-old customs. Recently, Oxfam has claimed that the lifestyle of the Maasai should be embraced as a response to climate change because of their eco-friendly practices and ability to farm in deserts and srublands.

> *Cows are awesome !*
> *I love cow pictures! Cows are fantastic animals! They're so calm and kind-looking, and they have beautiful eyes...*
> *I love being around them and talking to them... (I'm very talkative, and they're the only ones that listen without getting bored!)*
> *Joseph Moore, Louisville*

Traditional Maasai lifestyle centers around their cows. The measure of a man's wealth is in terms of cows and children. They believe that God gave them all the cows on earth. Young boys are sent out with the calves as soon as they can toddle.

The staple diet of the Maasai consists of cow's milk and maize-meal. The milk is largely drunk fresh or as fermented milk or buttermilk - a by-product of butter making. Butter is used in cooking and it is also an important infant food. Studies by the International Livestock Centre for Africa shows that about one litre of milk is consumed per person daily and milk consumption figures are very high by any standards. The needs for protein and essential amino acids are more than adequately satisfied. Electrocardiogram tests applied to 400 young adult males found no evidence whatsoever of heart disease, abnormalities or malfunction. Further study with carbon-14 tracers showed that the average cholesterol level was about 50 percent of that of an average American. These findings were ascribed to the their amazing fitness which was evaluated as "Olympic standard". Meat is consumed very irregularly and rarely.

For centuries, Maasai have lived alongside most wild animals and they have a strong aversion to eating game and birds. Maasai land now has East Africa's finest wildlife.

They are fierce when provoked, but easily moved to kindness when they hear of suffering and injustice.

When Kimeli Naiyomah tells his fellow villagers about the tragedy in America that has brought a nation to its knees, the villagers are so moved by this young man's story that they give some of their most precious possessions to the American people.

Thus in June of 2002, a very unusual ceremony begins in a far-flung village in western Kenya.

An American diplomat is surrounded by hundreds of Maasai people. A gift is about to be bestowed on the American men, women, and children, and he is there to accept it. The gift is as unsought and unexpected as it is extraordinary. A mere nine months have passed since the September 11 attacks, and hearts are raw. Tears flow freely from American and Maasai as these legendary warriors offer their gift to a grieving people half a world away.

Killing the cows and spoiling the land will not solve the problem of food. This is not civilization. Uncivilized men living in the jungle and being unqualified to produce food by agriculture and cow protection may eat animals, but a perfect human society advanced in knowledge must learn how to produce first-class food simply by agriculture and protection of cows.
~Srila Prabhupada (Lecture on Srimad Bhagavatam 10.7.13-15)

Word of the gift will travel news wires around the globe. Many will be profoundly touched, but for Americans, this selfless gesture will have deeper meaning still. For a heartsick nation, the gift of fourteen cows emerges from the choking dust and darkness as a soft light of hope—and friendship.

A **Bestseller Book**

Carmen Agra Deedy, a storyteller and author, saw the story and photograph of Maasai women in The New York Times, carrying a hand-lettered sign that read, "We give these cows to help you, September 11 tragedy." She did not lift her eyes from the print until she had read the article through to its end.

This inspired her to write the story book, 14 Cows for America, in collaboration with Kemeli Naiyomah. Thomas Gonzalez agreed to do the paintings for the book, which came out stunningly beautiful with rich hues of oranges and browns, and blues and greens, capturing the modest nobility of the Maasai people and the distinctive landscape of the African plain. Carmen Deedy hits all the right notes in this elegant story of generosity that crosses boundaries, nations, and cultures.

Curious cows checking out a new water pump in a ditch in their farm

The book was hailed as a must-read book for anyone. Not just for this day, but for any day. The sparse text and gorgeous dark and richly-colored illustrations of Thomas Gonzalez amplified the message. It was more than a tale of September 11. It was a portrait of humanity, and how we are all connected. Schoolchildren in America will be told for years how one day, thousands of miles away in Kenya, the continuation of life was celebrated with a most precious gift.

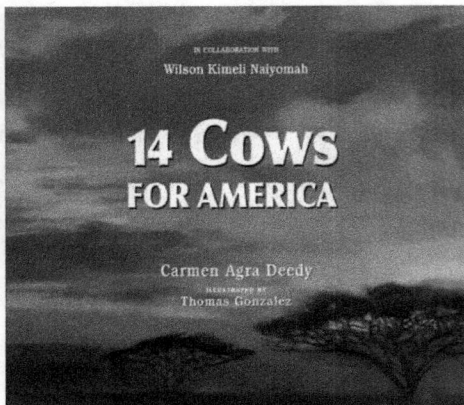

The flag commemorating the 14 Cows is hanging in the September 11 Memorial and Museum.

But would America, the land of hamburgers, also take up the Maasai spirit of protecting cows and nature along with their gifts?

Or will these cows also end up at Mcdonalds?

37.
Ganga's Story

I'm Ganga Jal, a Guernsey cow named after the holy water of the River Ganges. But my story doesn't start in India—it begins in Wisconsin, USA.

My mother, Goldie Goldstar, was born there on a dairy farm owned by the Proctor family. When the Proctors moved to Florida they brought my mom along. After some time in the South, however, the Proctors realized that they couldn't keep Goldie anymore. Not wanting to sell her to a commercial dairy (knowing well what her eventual fate would be), they asked their vet if he knew anyone who would take her. Fortunately for my mom, this vet knew about Save the Cow at the Krishna farm in nearby Alachua.

The Proctors asked the Save the Cow people if they would let Goldie live out her natural life on their farm. If so, the Proctors would give Goldie to them with only a few strings attached. You see, the Proctors had a teenage daughter, Jane, who was a member of the local 4-H club. She wanted to show Goldie at the county fair. So, string number one was that Jane could bring my mom the fair every year. String number two was that Goldie would be bred and if a female was born she too could go the county fair with Jane. Luckily for my mom (and for me), Save the Cow agreed to the proposal and Goldie Goldstar moved onto the farm. She was even given the Krishna name, Gauri (Sanskrit for Golden One), so she would fit into the herd.

My Mom And Me

When fall arrived, Jane and the Proctors came and took my mom to the county fair. Unfortunately, Goldie had a bump on her back that marred her bovine beauty (at least in the eyes of the dairy cow judges) and, as a result, she never won any prizes for Jane. So all hope was put in the next generation—that's where I come into the picture.

My mother became pregnant by some strange method called AI (that's artificial insemination, not artificial intelligence) and nine months later, on April 2, 2000, I was born (making me an Aires). Since cows can live to about twenty, a human year is about five cow years (as compared to dog years, which I understand have a 7:1 ratio). That makes my age about 40, in human years, that is. By the way, I am the youngest member of the Save the Cow herd. You see, and this may sound funny, Save the Cow is a Florida community for retired and rescued cows. But the history of Save the Cow is another story for another day.

(Save The Cow is a charity working for cow protection. It is based in Alachua, Fl, USA)

106

38.

Cows Form Cliques!

By Marji

Scientists long ago (and by long ago, I mean 2005) discovered cattle form cliques and even go so far as to hold grudges. I've seen that in the herd of cows, bulls and calves who live next to the sanctuary and are, tragically, raised for consumption. There are probably 3-4 different sub-groups amongst the eighty some odd cattle, and they generally do not mix company. Except for the bulls who are equal opportunity flirters. My favorite sub-sub group is comprised of Long Face, Skinny Cow and White Tail. Yes, silly names, but I have a hard time getting even more personal than that. Long Face is a beautiful brown-brindle cow with a loooong white-blazed face. Skinny Cow is a smaller, slender, black cow and White Tail is a black cow with white tail-hair. They do not hang out with anyone else - it's just them and their calves. Sometimes they'll be standing twenty feet from their sub-group with their backs turned, snubbing the rest. When they get separated, they'll moo for hours, guiding the lost cow back to her small clan.

At the sanctuary, there are five cattle - Sadie, Howie, Nicholas, Summer and Freedom. They're a tight-knit group and I can't say they bear any grudges toward one another. Sadie is enamored with Howie and rarely leaves his side, while Nicholas, Summer and Freedom sometimes spend time frolicking away from the two older bovines. This is all besides the point, which is that I learned first-

A healthy cow gives about 200,000 glasses of milk in her lifetime. Cows produce 90% of the milk in the world. Rest 10% comes from goats, sheep, buffalo, camels etc.

hand what a cow-grudge entails.

Every day, I like to go out and see Sadie. I've worked hard to build up a positive relationship with her, often around food. So I usually bring her an apple or two and tell her she is a Very Nice Cow while I brush her. I always make sure to pay attention to all the other cattle, because I love them too. But I rarely bring them apples. Yesterday, Howie had had enough. He would not talk to me at all. Every time I tried to scratch his big neck, he turned away. Panic!!

Mulling his behavior over, I decided to bring him an apple the next day. In fact, I brought out five apples, one for each cow. Sadie's eyes got real huge, thinking she had scored in the apple-eating department. As she scarfed down her apple, I approached Howie - he eyed me warily but stretched out his head to inspect the apple. Taking it gently in his mouth, he rolled it around and then he *spit it back out at me*. This seemed like an attempt at insulting my apple selecting abilities, so I let him taste-test each apple. He spit them all out. Fine, be that way. Nicholas got a Howie-spit drenched apple while Summer and Freedom thought the apples were a rather silly thing to try and eat. Sadie nudged me, demanding that I stop trying to share HER apples and give them to HER. So I did. Howie felt it was the opportune time to amble over, nearly crushing my foot, and demand attention. He let me scratch and brush him thoroughly. So I guess I was forgiven? I'm not sure, but I hope to remain in his good graces; being snubbed by a bovine buddy is no fun.

(These cows live in Animal Place Sanctuary, California, USA)

39.

Cowlick

The Way To Give 'Solace'

By Sarah Rath

O ur daughter's name was Christine, but we called her 'Tootsie'. She was two years old at the time and her big brother, Mark, was three and a half.

One summer afternoon Mark came running, screaming, to tell us that Tootsie was stuck. He pulled us to the far back yard where we found she was, indeed, 'stuck'.

She had placed her head through the square-wire fence of the pasture and the 'friendly' cow was licking her face.

Tootsie's screams could have reached downtown, and she had good reason. Have you ever felt the coarseness of a cow's tongue?"

Harder she screamed, harder the cow licked her face, just to solace the poor girl.

(Rath, Sarah. *About Cows. Minocqua, WI:* NorthWood Press, Inc., 1987)

I have loved cows since I was born!
Cows are awesome creatures and should be treated just like us, but better!
No hamburgers! Milking is ok but thats it!
~Juliette P, Sweden

40.

Story of Sadie

The Face of Modern Dairy Industry

By Marji

Sadie is special, at least to me. She is the face of the dairy industry, those beautiful cows who are bred and milked, bred and milked in a cycle of loss and separation. In her life, she gave birth to four calves, their fates intertwined with her own. Each calf was a marker of loss for Sadie, torn from her at birth. She did not nurse or groom them; she never watched from a distance as they frolicked in green pastures. There was never a time when she met grand-calves, the young of her own daughters.

Her sons, sweet and smart, gentle and curious, they are all dead now. Sold at auction for $5-15, raised and slaughtered for veal or cheap dairy beef. None of them made it past the age of two.

Some of her daughters are alive, no doubt. Others are dead, slaughtered and disassembled for what meager flesh humans can obtain from their overworked bodies.

She spent six years at a dairy farm. Six years of producing gallon after gallon of breast milk for another species. Every meaningful behavior, from reproductive choice to nursing her own young to choosing what and where to eat, all of them denied.

And when her production decreased, when an infection common

to 50-70% of all dairy cows invaded her mammary glands - suddenly she was no longer a valuable commodity. She had never been seen as *someone*, an animal with interests of her very own, but as a *something*, a unit of production whose worth was measured in gallons.

She was sent to auction. That awful place where other sentient beings are paraded in front of humans, where they are watched from bleachers, where they piss and shit in fear, where they cry. And where they go unheard. She was purchased by a veterinary university and used as a teaching tool. Her mastitis was left untreated, yet another chapter of exploitation.

Someone saw her as an individual and ached for her. They saw a sweet animal who was struggling to survive amidst poking and prodding and a painful medical condition. It was an orchestrated production of frustration trying to convince the university to release her to the sanctuary. But in the end, she arrived, shy and concerned, an udder that sank nearly to her knees, a sign of human cruelty, of every meat eater's complicity in her suffering.

I will be honest, Sadie is never going to like humans. It has taken me years to touch her, to scratch her face like a bovine friend would. She tolerates my presence because I am a known entity, a biped who has given her apples and massages and has yet to do anything to violate the tentative trust built.

Her mastitis took years to heal. Years. It was only through not milking her, through the painful removal of cup after cup of pus and infection did it heal. And it was only because her caregivers, people who wanted nothing more than for her to get better, had to confine her, force her to suffer even more indignities. She endured,

Cows are extremely maternal animals and both the mother cow and the baby calf suffer terribly from being separated at such a young age. In fact, one cow missed her baby so much that she broke out of her paddock and trekked through 8 kilometers of paddocks and rivers to find her baby. On dairy farms, mother cows can be heard bellowing out wildly trying to find their babies as well as running after the cattle trucks that take their babies to separate farms.

unwillingly, and it pained us to watch.

Life for Sadie now is one of choices. Like where to graze or nap. Or what to do with herself at ten in the morning. Or whether she wants to hang out with the other cattle or lie in the compost pile on her own. When we take in male calves from the dairy industry, the unwanted *by-product*s, she decides whether they get a facial grooming or a back grooming. There are still times when we take decisions away from her, like when she needs hoof trims or pain medication. We hope that these are minor inconveniences and her life is generally full of good, positive, enriching experiences. She deserves them.

University of Saskatchewan researcher Jon Watts notes that cows who are kept in groups of more than 200 get confused, scared and constantly fight for dominance . This is akin to how humans would feel if we were penned in a tiny space with thousands of unfamiliar people. Just like us, cows like to be near their families and friends.

Sadie will be turning 11 this March. She has been at the sanctuary for four years and has really blossomed from a shy, abused dairy cow to a lover of back scratches and apples.

(Sadie lives in Animal Place Sanctuary, California, USA)

According to Vedic conception, the animals, they are also members of your family. Because they are giving service. Not that one section of the members of my family I give protection, and the other section, I take everything from them and then cut throat. This is not civilization. You keep your sons, wife, daughters, cows, dogs, they are animals, asses, domestic animals, horses, elephants. If you are rich, you can keep elephants also. It does not mean... Either family-wise or state-wise, it does not mean that you give protection to some members and cut throat of the others. Oh, how horrible it is.
~Srimad Bhagavatam (Bhagavad-gita 1.26-27, London, July 21, 1973)

41.

Cows Have Strange Sixth Sense

Researchers at a German University used Google Earth to find that cows tended to face north-south along the Earth's magnetic field lines while grazing or resting.

Past research has shown that wind and sunlight can cause herd animals such as cows to change their alignment, depending on the conditions. Researchers used Google Earth satellite images to see how cows align themselves in a magnetic north-south direction while grazing or resting. These images confirmed that herds of cattle tend to face in the north-south direction of Earth's magnetic lines.

Staring at cows may not equal the thrill of spotting celebrities in public or gawking at car accidents, but the researchers found nonetheless that our bovine friends display this strange sixth sense for direction.

"Google Earth is perfect for this kind of research, because the animals are undisturbed by the observer," says Sabine Begall, a zoologist at the University of Duisburg-Essen in Germany and coauthor on the study detailed in the journal *Proceedings of the National Academy of Sciences*.

Wind and time of day did not offer better explanations for why 8,510 cows in 308 locations around the world would mostly face north-south. Shadows suggested that many of the images were taken on cloudless, sunny days, so Begall's group also factored in direct ground observations of cattle herds.

A strong wind or sunlight on a cold day have typically proved more the "exceptions to the rule" that might cause large animals to face away from magnetic north-south.

In Czech Republic, researchers also examined fresh beds left by resting cows in the snow and alignment was the same. Cows face a more magnetic north-south direction rather than geographic north-south, (Earth's magnetic poles do not line up perfectly with the North and South Poles).

Previous research has shown that animals such as birds, turtles and salmon migrate using a sense of magnetic direction, and small mammals such as rodents and one bat species also have a magnetic compass. Begall and fellow researchers became interested in seeing if larger mammals possessed a similar magnetic sense.

"Our first idea was to study sleeping directions of humans (e.g. when doing camping), but there were too many constraints," says Begall. "So, the idea arose to look for other large mammals like cows, and we were fascinated when we recognized that cows could

be found on Google Earth satellite images."

Google Earth's convenience also came with some downsides. The researchers could not distinguish between head and rear for some of the cows because of low image resolutions. However, the researchers suggest that the finding of large animals' sense of magnetic direction could raise other agricultural questions, such as whether keeping cows in barns facing east-west might affect milk production.

Q: Where do baby cows go for lunch?
A: To a calf-a tiria!

42.

Cows Are Precious

Canadian Cow Goes For $1.2 Million

In November 2009, Missy, a 3 year-old dairy cow was sold for $1.2 million at Toronto's annual Royal Agricultural Winter Fair.

Missy is the second cow in Canada to hit the million dollar mark.

Missy is from Morsan Farms, near the town of Ponoka, in Alberta, Canada. She was bought jointly at the auction by two buyers, from the U.S. and Denmark. Due to her natural genetic superiority, she could have as many as 75 calves over the course of her life.

The oldest cow ever recorded in Western world was a cow named "Big Bertha" that died 3 months short of her 49th birthday on New Years Eve, 1993.
Big Bertha also holds the record for lifetime breeding as she produced 39 calves.

43.

Ignorance

A Prerequisite of The Standard Western Diet

By *Sienna Parker*

I think parents either want to "protect" children by not telling them where meat comes from (since most children have a natural love for animals), or eating meat is so automatic for the parents, that they don't even think to explain it to their children. I wish my parents had told me earlier where meat came from.

I help out with a school garden club. Of the eight children (all between 5 and 12) who attended yesterday, not one could identify the vegetable we were harvesting. It was a leek.

I guess ignorance is a prerequisite of the standard Western diet.

My sister was fairly young when she learned where her favourite food, beef, came from. She didn't understand the concept, however of how we got the meat from the cows. She assumed the meat were the "spots" (the ones seen on cows used for dairy) on the cows and when the meat was "ripe" it would fall off and the farmers would go out into the field to gather it.

Sadly, when she discovered this was not how things were done and that the cows had to be killed for her to enjoy their meat, she was upset for the longest time. She was young and didn't have any control over her diet at that age. She has long since forgotten this.

It seems a lot of vegetarians learned where meat comes from at a young age. Perhaps this is what helped them to make the change. I was 4 when my mum told me that animals were killed for meat. I can clearly remember that moment and how I felt. I was shocked and couldn't believe the awfulness of what she was telling me. I even thought this cannot be true. I only kept eating meat until I was 13 because I didn't like vegetables but the seed was planted the moment I found out.

(Sienna Parker is a vegetarian and lives in Catalonia, Spain)

Cow's Human Friends

"My friends are all badgers,

or leopards or wolves,

or foxes, or eagles, and how

can I ever reveal

to such glamorous folk

that I'm only a Brown Swiss cow?"

-Sarah Rath

44.

Inseparable Friends

A Calf And A Goat

R oyal Society for the Prevention of Cruelty to Animals
(RSPCA) is a charity in England that promotes animal
welfare, especially of cats and dogs. It runs an animal shelter at
Fairfield.

Recently RSPCA staff faced an unusual problem after a love affair
developed between a curious calf and a lonely goat in the Fairfield
animal shelter.

Barnaby, the cow and
Sprout, the goat were
brought in to the
RSPCA's shelter
separately and have
been inseparable ever
since.

Where the calf goes,
Sprout, the goat
follows. They sleep
together, eat together and Sprout quickly retreats behind Barnaby's
broad hide if he's threatened by any other animals.

Even though there are other goats in the yard, this goat turns his
back on his own kind, preferring his bovine mate.

Both the calf and the goat were brought to the animal shelter as
stray homeless animals. The goat was emaciated and suffering from
tick paralysis. But within a day or two of meeting at the shelter, the

duo struck a friendship. Now both are purely into each other.

RSPCA officer Justin Palazzo says the pair is inseparable, "It's a strange thing but we see them following each other around all the time. Sprout prefers to hang out with Barnaby. It's strange. There's other goats there but he just turns his nose up at them. We are trying and keep them together."

Oh Sacred Cow
If you ask me
India is the place to be
There cows are sacred
none are objects of hatred
There cows roam free
-G. Vincent

45.

What Do Cows Drink?

A Riddle

There is an old trick you can try on your friends. Get a person to say "Silk" then "Milk" repeatedly, about ten times each, and then after saying "Silk" for the last time you ask, "What do cows drink?" And the person always says "Milk".

And then you say, "No they don't, cow's drink water."

Not particularly clever, really, but there it is.

A person did this trick with his seven-year old daughter one day and, after telling that cows drink water, she stopped, and screwed up her nose, and thought for a while.

"But when they're young they drink milk," she argued.

Again, no great revelation there, but it was interesting to note he did this trick hundreds of times over thirty years, to adults, grandparents, uncles, aunties, school-friends, girl-friends etc., but his daughter was the first person to question the conclusion.

In any case, cows drink water and eat dry grass and leave all the good milk for our usage. Cows are magnanimous souls!

One should accept only those things that are set aside by the Lord as his quota. The cow, for instance, gives milk, but she does not drink that milk: she eats grass and straw, and her milk is designated as food for human beings. Such is the arrangement of the Lord. ~ Isopanisad 1

121

46.

Suddenly In Fashion

Farming and Cows

Farming, which many city folk once associated primarily with rustic farmers and boring chores is suddenly in vogue. Never mind that most of the food we eat comes not from cozy acreages but from big corporate operations. Never mind that census data tell us that fewer than half of family-run farms show a positive net income (in other words, most farmers need day jobs). Even though farming no longer quite makes it as "a way of life," it's somehow become the next best thing (or maybe an even better thing): a lifestyle.

Farming is suddenly in fashion.

Some time back, Huffington Post, a popular news site in America featured a photo gallery of "hot organic farmers". The response was so overwhelming that it did yet another spread. From a pallid hipster growing organic vegetables on a Brooklyn rooftop to a husky Californian whose specialty lettuce crops are bathed in golden sunlight, the photos suggest that running a farm — at least the kind that appears far removed from pesticides and corporate contracts — is very similar to modeling for a hot catalog.

"We think organic farmers are rock stars and heroes," the site says. "And nothing is trendier than someone who likes to get dirty and supports the great food revolution." Readers are encouraged to vote on their favorite farmer. Forget rock star: Farmers are so hot they could date rock stars. To some it is refreshing to see that farmers are glamorized in the media instead of, say, strippers.

But no reality show or Internet photo gallery can compare with the most unexpected Internet craze in recent memory: FarmVille. Launched on Facebook last June by the video-game developer Zynga, the social game now has nearly 60 million users, making it the most popular game on Facebook and, according to Zynga, the fastest-growing social game of all time.

Internet social games are well known to be habit-forming, but a recent spate of news coverage has suggested that FarmVille is roughly as enslaving as heroin. Users report missing work, abandoning friends and setting their alarms to wake up several times during the night so they can make the moves necessary to advance in the game.

And what particular thrills do those moves generate? Harvesting crops, milking cows of course! And buying seed and livestock and trees and buildings with virtual coins (extra coins can be purchased with real-life credit cards). And helping neighboring farmers with chores. And getting really excited because a cow wandered onto your farm.

After creating an avatar, a player is given six plots of land and the opportunity to cultivate various food products, some of which grow in a matter of hours and will wilt if not harvested on time (thus the need to get up in the middle of the night). Roaming animals such as a pink cow that produces strawberry milk and an ugly duckling that turns into a swan can be adopted and cultivated for profit (in a loving, free-range sort of way). Looks like tens of millions of people are losing sleep over virtual crop rotation.

Other than this game, there is outrage of agribusiness companies over Michelle Obama's organic garden who fear that an organic vegetable patch in every yard may become the Obama administration's version of "a chicken in every pot."

Are we to infer from the FarmVille phenomenon that people are finally switching their allegiances from urban-industrial environs to lifestyles of being closer to Mother Earth? Are people yearning to connect back with mother nature, land and cows? Are people tired of techno-industrial setup and looking for something thats natural for their soul - a life founded on land and cows?

"I asked the waiter, 'Is this milk fresh?' He said, 'Lady, three hours ago it was grass"
- Phyllis Diller

47.

Cow Fashion Show

In India cows were treated as family members and never as pieces of meat. On festive occasions, cows would be decorated just as other family children. Some places in India, this tradition is still being practiced.

One such festive occasion is Sankranti. This year in Bangalore, Radio Mirchi, a popular Radio channel, presented a cow fashion show at the local ISKCON temple.

Ten teams of three each from colleges of Bangalore strove to dress up cows with themes varying from the basic 'Gow Mata' by the Sindhi College to an 'Astronaut Theme' from Seshadhripuram College, covering diverse subjects that included Indian bridal dress to global warming and eco-friendliness.

The team from Vogue Fashion Institute (VFI) was awarded the first prize for its "Beauty and the Beast' theme. The first runner up was also a team from VFI with an 'anti-plastic' theme. The second runner-up was the "Astronaut Theme'. Many other colleges participated in the show.

The station had been announcing the contest on air for some time, and, of the twenty five teams that applied, ten were shortlisted based on innovativeness of the theme that they proposed.

48.

This One Was My Bodyguard

By Michelle Evans

It's normally thought that cows are dumb - and may be some of them are (I've only known a few).

But on the summer farm we had a cow that adored me (and I her) ... and my much older brother and I were in the pasture when he was beating the pooey out of me - and she literally came trundling full speed and butted him full force! Knocked him right off his feet and then thunked him a good one with her head while he was down!

And then came over to me and licked my face and hair. (You have to love a cow before you find that huge wet raspy tongue a comfort!)

Yup, I can't help but think if an animal (even a huge lumbering cow) is given love they will return it.

~Michelle Evans, British Columbia, Canada

Cows are empathetic and socially sensitive animals. A cattle herd is a community, and its members rely on each other for a range of emotional needs. For example, studies show that cows are less stressed by unfamiliar circumstances when they are with cows they know. They eat less feed when other cows they associate with closely are stressed. And when they are separated from the herd, their behavior becomes restless and their levels of the stress hormone cortisol spike.
~ "The Social Behaviour of Cattle", Marie-France Bouissou et al. (Saskatoon: CABI Publishing, 2001).

Appendix

Steps You Can Take To Protect and Serve Mother Cow

(Some of the following are excerpts from the Author's earlier book, 'Cow And Humanity - Made For Each Other')

The first step in cow protection would be to stop eating them. Of course, in many cultures like Hindus of India, abstaining from beef is already in practice.

Every household can adopt a cow or can feel responsible for the livelihood of a cow. It does not necessarily mean personally taking care but it could be sponsoring a cow in one of the organizations that look after cows.

Traditional Hindus had many interesting practices related to cow protection which one may adapt as far as possible. Many families still continue their tradition in this regard.

In many homes, the first chapati (Indian bread) they cook is kept aside for cows. Since cooking is done at least twice a day, cows get a minimum of two chapatis from each family. The offering to God or saying grace is done with the second chapati. This means the cow's share precedes that of God's. Also vegetable and fruit peels and other leftovers are carefully collected for feeding them. Jaggery and molasses are their favorites and many families keep sufficient stock of these.

On social occasions like childbirth, marriage or bereavement, a portion of expenditure is dedicated towards cow protection. But these days billions of rupees are spent in lavish Hindu ceremonies like marriages but not a penny is spared for this cause. It was a tradition to seek the blessings of cow and bull on these auspicious occasions. When some one in the family fell sick, a cow would be fed and a prayer would be offered for quick recovery. Also water was kept in front of the house for stray cows and other animals and birds.

It was believed that a family would be comfortable if it kept its cows comfortably. A society's well-being was gauged by the well-being of the cows. Vedic literatures mention that an entire family or nation can be doomed if the cows are in distress. If this is true than today's society is unhappy because it has failed in its duty of cow protection.

Also it was common to set aside a certain percentage of income for the cows. Many families even now set aside one rupee a day for this purpose. When famine strikes, some families go out of their way to take care of the cows. It is not uncommon to find skinny human beings and well-fed cows. Traditionally, old cows and bulls were looked after just like old parents, with entire family tending to their needs.

Traditional educational system, taught in the gurukulas, emphasized the importance of cow protection. Today's educational system discusses the benefits of cow slaughter and beef export. India is already a world leader in beef export. Many Brazilian and Australian companies are unable to compete and going bankrupt.

The virtue of kindness has to be inculcated from a tender age. Cow protection needs to be included in the standard curriculum. If Garuda (bird carrier of Lord Vishnu) can be the national symbol of an Islamic country like Indonesia, cow can definitely be the national animal of India.

In India, cow protection remains a hotly debated issue. Many organizations are struggling to get cow slaughter completely banned while the government is trying to modernize slaughterhouses and augment beef export earnings.

If cow keeping becomes economically viable, that will immediately stop cow slaughter in India. Farmers often sell their cattle unwillingly out of economic pressure. If people start using cow products like toothpaste, soaps, medicines, fertilizers, pesticides etc., there will be no more cows available for slaughter.

Main utility of cow is her dung and urine. Milk was always considered a byproduct. Today cow's main function is to provide milk and meat.

Leaving aside all cow products, if Indians just take two spoons of cow urine distillate every morning, it will save many cows and health of the nation will improve dramatically. In turn it will save billions in health care. Cow based rural economy is the only way to go for the third world countries like India. That's the only way the village economies can flourish and the masses can rise above the poverty line.

Cow is a mobile dispensary. Over 150 medicines are being manufactured out of cow products now. These medicines, known as 'panchagavya chikitsa' work like a charm.

This is the only viable system of medicine for Indian masses. Modern health care is a failure even in a country like America where it remains a hotly debated issue. Health care is a multi-trillion dollar industry with strong muscle and lobbying power. India in next five years is investing $216 billion in health care infrastructure but it will remain out of reach for over 90% of the population. Health care system based on cow products is cheap and effective. It is highly suitable for rural masses who have easy access to cows. Panchagavya centers can be established on village level not only in India but all over the third world.

Now many medical colleges have started courses on panchagavya and dedicated cow science universities (called Kamdhenu visvavidyalaya) are coming up.

Cow is the single fact which can unite numerous factions of Hinduism. No matter what is one's path, every Hindu agrees on the universal practice of cow protection. In Hinduism, different schools of philosophical thought exist and some of them don't see each other eye to eye. But still there is complete agreement on one point - cow protection.

Today's younger generation is blamed for not showing enough respect to elders. In traditional India, children were taught to respect mother cow and bull from an early age and this training extended to their original parents. As old cows and bulls are slaughtered now, a time will come when old parents would similarly be killed and their organs exported.

Every town and village in India had cow service cooperatives known as pinjarapoles. Retired cows passed their last days there in comfort and dignity. The local communities organized and executed this on a cooperative basis.

No cow should be left to loiter on Indian streets. They lead a very miserable life. Suffering from hunger, thirst and disease, they are often injured by moving vehicles. How can any sane person turn a blind eye to such a pathetic sight. Every town and city should have veterinary hospital for sick and injured cows. *CareforCows.org* is doing a commendable work in this connection in Vraja area of north India. In Delhi and NCR area, *Love4cow Trust* is spearheading the efforts in caring for stray cows. They have a truck with hydraulic system to carry sick or injured cows. Similar facilities are required for every Indian town and city.

Biogas and fertilizer from cow dung represent humanity's future when the fossil fuels run out. A large family can meet all its requirement of energy and fertilizer from just two cows. Every home can be self-sufficient and grow energy in its own backyard.

Production techniques of various cow products should be made available on village level to make it a widespread cottage industry. Government can subsidize the machinery and investment just as it subsidizes slaughterhouses and beef production.

A nationwide awareness has to be created. Citizens should vote for a political party which has cow protection in its agenda. All kingdoms in India set aside a portion of state outlay towards cow protection. Today's government is dedicating its resources for killing

Sometimes the naughty babies (Krishna and Balarama) would crawl up to the cowshed, catch the tail of a calf and stand up. The calves, being disturbed, would immediately begin running here and there, and the children would be dragged over clay and cow dung. To see this fun, Yasoda and Rohini would call all their neighborhood friends, the gopis. Upon seeing these childhood pastimes of Lord Krsna, the gopis would be merged in transcendental bliss. In their enjoyment they would laugh very loudly. ~ Krishna Book (Ch 8, Vision of the Universal Form)

more and more cows.

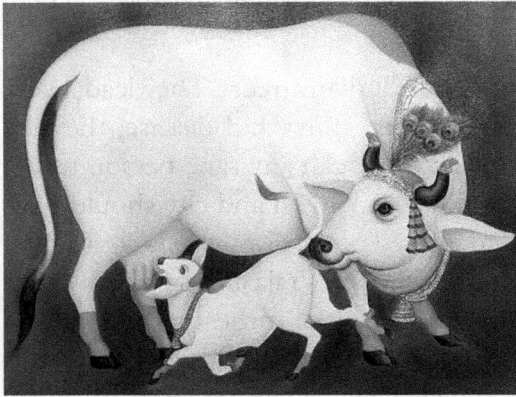

Murder is one thing but a murder involving exceptional brutality or cruelty is a whole different thing. For days and weeks on end, cows are piled on top of one another and shipped to far distant places. Most of them are injured and many die. Its long cruel road to the slaughterhouse. This is their final journey after a lifetime of service. This is the reward these innocent creatures receive after giving so much to the human race. The treatment they receive is the last frontier of inhumanity. A public awareness has to be created against this barbarism and culprits should be brought to book. Cruel transport is illegal but the police is always hand in gloves with the butchers.

Cow is also a mobile temple. She is said to house the Supreme Lord and all the functional deities of material world. Cows and bulls are represented in all Hindu temples and home altars.

There is need for more seminars and workshops on the subject, both on local and international level.

If we examine the world history in last two thousand years, we find that all the revolutions were inspired by literature. There is need for more printed material on the subject to reach every home. Also there is need for more material for world wide web.

Things Can And Do Change With Efforts

A lot of things have been changed in this world with effort. There is no need to think that "nothing" can ever be done to stop the cruelty on cows and other animals.

Previously, there was no concern at all for animal testing on products, for example. The majority of people did not even know their products where being tested on animals.

Well, now they do. PETA called attention to it, and brought about enforced labeling on products that test on animals (among other things).

That's just a small example. Slavery used to exist in the world. Now, no one would even consider it. Something/someone changed it. It didn't just happen by itself. If enough people care and work together, anything can be changed.

It's like trying to turn the Titanic around, getting people to think of cow as friend, not food, but hopefully in the future it will be a thing of the past, like slavery and such.

THE AUTHOR

Dr. Sahadeva dasa (Sanjay Shah), is a monk in vaisnava tradition. Coming from a prominent family of Rajasthan, he graduated in commerce from St.Xaviers College, Kolkata and then went on to complete his CA (Chartered Accountancy) and ICWA (Cost and works Accountancy) with national ranks. Later he received his doctorate.

For close to last two decades, he is leading a monk's life and he has made serving God and humanity as his life's mission. His areas of work include research in Vedic and contemporary thought, Corporate and educational training, social work and counselling, travelling in India and aborad, writing books and of course, practicing spiritual life and spreading awareness about the same.

He is also an accomplished musician, composer, singer, instruments player and sound engineer. He has more than a dozen albums to his credit so far. (SoulMelodies.com) His varied interests include alternative holistic living, vedic studies, social criticism, environment, linguistics, history, art & crafts, nature studies, web technologies etc.

His earlier books, Oil - A Global Crisis and Its Solutions (oilCrisisSolutions.com), End of Modern Civilization and Alternative future (WorldCrisisSolutions.com) have been acclaimed internationally. More information about his works is available on his portal DrDasa.com.

By The Same Author

Oil-Final Countdown To A Global Crisis And Its Solutions

End of Modern Civilization And Alternative Future

To Kill Cow Means To End Human Civilization

Cow And Humanity - Made For Each Other

Cows Are Cool - Love 'Em!

Capitalism Communism And Cowism - A New Economics For The 21st Century

Noble Cow - Munching Grass, Looking Curious And Just Hanging Around

Let's Be Friends - A Curious, Calm Cow

Wondrous Glories of Vraja

We Feel Just Like You Do

Tsunami of Diseases Headed Our Way - Know Your Food Before Time Runs Out

Cow Killing And Beef Export - The Master Plan To Turn India Into A Desert By 2050

(More information on availability : DrDasa.com)

www.ingramcontent.com/pod-product-compliance
Lightning Source LLC
Chambersburg PA
CBHW060503280326
41933CB00014B/2846